"Eugene Petersen once said, 'It is hard being myself, by myself.' *Ubuntu* is a popular phrase in South Africa that means 'We are, therefore I am.' Jim Putman gets this profound truth about our design by God as relational beings and provides a path for us to discover it with power in our 'all about me' culture."

—**Randy Frazee**, senior minister of Oak Hills Church; author of *The Connecting Church 2.0*

"Jim Putman helpfully shows us that the 'Just Jesus and me' attitude of so many Christians is not only unbiblical but soul destroying and faith killing. Discipleship happens in relationships, period. As Jim points out, all the fruits of the Spirit are others-related. This book not only paints a positive, compelling vision for Christian community, it charts the way forward. Both pastors and dissatisfied Christians will find this book a refreshing, practical, and helpful read."

—**J.D. Greear**, pastor of The Summit Church in Raleigh-Durham, North Carolina; author of *Stop Asking Jesus into Your Heart*

"Jim is known for his commitment to Jesus's relational method for disciple making. But in this book he challenges the definition of spiritual maturity most accepted in the American church. He asks and answers the question, what is spiritual maturity? He makes the point that most Christians are not experiencing all that Jesus has for them, and the result is a faith that does not satisfy th———— re-ate stability in a shaky wo————————————— st. This book gives everyone a —————————————— ks each of us questions that w ——————————————— s.

Jim's advice in this book can help you be all that Jesus desires you to be and help the church become a light in a dark world again."

—**Josh McDowell**, author and speaker

"Through humor, pain, life experience, and a biblical foundation, *The Power of Together* will raise your vision to new heights for the power of relationships in God's family. Jim Putman will inspire you to fight for authentic, life-giving, and soul-building relationships."

—**Gene Appel**, senior pastor of Eastside Christian Church

"Jim Putman's *The Power of Together* touched me deeply. Most of the mistakes people make in attempting to be a disciple is to think information is the key to transformation. No one believes more in the power of Scripture and is more faithful than Jim to preach it. But what the people from afar don't see is Jim's commitment to relationships, how he lives it, and how powerful they are. This book plumbs the depth of the human soul in a simple, powerful way. You can't read this book without changing—I know it ministered deeply to me. "

—**Bill Hull**, author of *Conversion & Discipleship: You Can't Have One without the Other*; leader of The Bonhoeffer Project

THE POWER of TOGETHER

DISCOVER THE CHRISTIAN LIFE
YOU'VE BEEN MISSING

JIM PUTMAN

BakerBooks
a division of Baker Publishing Group
Grand Rapids, Michigan

Published by Baker Books
a division of Baker Publishing Group
P.O. Box 6287, Grand Rapids, MI 49516-6287
www.bakerbooks.com

Printed in the United States of America

Library of Congress Cataloging-in-Publication Data
Names: Putman, Jim, 1966– author.
Title: The power of together : discover the Christian life you've been missing / Jim Putman.
Description: Grand Rapids : Baker Books, 2016. | Includes bibliographical references.
Identifiers: LCCN 2016003927 | ISBN 9780801008009 (pbk.)
Subjects: LCSH: Fellowship—Religious aspects—Christianity. | Communities— Religious aspects—Christianity. | Interpersonal relations—Religious aspects— Christianity. | Spiritual formation.
Classification: LCC BV4517.5 .P88 2016 | DDC 248.4—dc23
LC record available at http://lccn.loc.gov/2016003927

Author is represented by WordServe Literary Group. (www.wordserveliterary.com)

16 17 18 19 20 21 22   7 6 5 4 3 2 1

To my parents,
Bill and Bobbi Putman,
who first showed me what discipleship
and real relationship look like.

Contents

1

Something Is Definitely Missing

As a former high school and college wrestler, I can tell you that I needed to learn to deal with pain. Few people understand what it takes to be a wrestler (the real kind—not WWE). The hard work, the extreme cardio endurance to maintain, the constant strain against joints, the jolting of the spine— all of it is painful, and for many athletes the pain becomes cumulative and lifelong.

Wrestlers must practice extreme discipline when it comes to diet and water intake as well. Every day they keep one eye on the fridge and one on the scale. They weigh in before every match, and sometimes they weigh in on multiple days in a row. After they weigh in, they eat like crazy to get strength to wrestle, and then they begin dieting again to "make weight" (achieve the optimum weight level for their wrestling classification) the next day. These days, most schools and wrestling programs have rules that make wrestling far healthier for those who participate, but back when I wrestled I would often fluctuate fifteen pounds a week during wrestling season. Practices such as these can lead to an unhealthy view of food for the rest of a wrestler's life.

One lasting effect of all that weight watching is that some former wrestlers want to eat and drink more than we need to, as we try to make up for years of missing Thanksgiving meals, Sunday dinners, and midnight Taco Bell runs. Since we didn't get to eat often when we wrestled, we developed the habit of being picky about food. When we did eat, it had to be food we really liked as well as substantial enough to get our bodies through the workouts. Why waste one of our few precious meals eating food we didn't like? Once I tasted something I loved, I didn't care to try something new. I particularly loved lasagna—specifically, my mother's lasagna. She always made it from the same recipe, and it was always perfect.

Putting all this together—the constant obsession I'd developed as a wrestler with eating, a pattern of eating only the exact food I liked because I'd grown picky, and a really good lasagna recipe from my mother—led to some interesting times when I was first married.

I was still wrestling competitively when Lori and I got married in college. One morning when my wife (who hadn't had a lot of experience cooking or with wrestlers) asked what I wanted for dinner that night, I told her about my favorite dinner, lasagna. My new bride smiled and told me she would fix it for me. After being far away from my parents' home for a while, and not eating much because I was in the middle of a wrestling season, I was thrilled. I thought about the upcoming dinner all day.

That night I came home to a wonderful wife who had slaved in the kitchen for hours to make what she thought was a masterpiece. She stood there smiling over a table already set. (Now, here is where it gets bad, but before I tell you what happened, remember I was a new husband and a brand-new believer, so please give me a break.) I forked up a big bite of lasagna and took a good hard look at it first. Immediately I noticed that it did not look the same as my mother's. I sniffed it. Nope. Didn't smell like my mother's either. Then I tasted it.

No, this definitely was not the right lasagna.

I even had the gall to tell my wife that fact. Lori's lasagna was not exactly *horrible*, but it definitely was not what I had expected. I hadn't learned how to fake liking something yet, nor how to be diplomatic. I tried to tell Lori that my mother was an expert lasagna maker, and I loved the precise way she cooked it. I tried to explain how anything less was just—*less*.

Fortunately, after she shed some tears, and after me cleaning up my relational mess, my wife came to understand that when I said "I like lasagna," I didn't mean just any old lasagna. I liked my mother's lasagna—only!

Over the years, my wife has become a great repeater of my mother's recipes, down to the last ingredient. And I have learned how to be a much more sensitive husband. But there is a greater point to all this talk about lasagna—I promise.

A plate of good lasagna is a picture of the way God intended us to live. God is the Master Designer and Expert Chef, and in the Bible He has given us a specific recipe that, if followed, will sustain and empower us over the years as a part of God's family. Not only that, but the enticing aroma of this delicious dish will attract others to join the family dinner. That's the good news. The bad news is that if we don't follow this recipe, we'll always be missing something we need and that God designed for us. Sure, we might be eating something, but it won't be God's *best*.

Of course, this analogy only goes so far. There was nothing bad or unhealthy about my wife's recipe. It was simply different than my mother's. However, in the spiritual world, only God's recipe has the ability to produce the life He intended for us. We also have an enemy who can deceive us into omitting something essential or even introduce a subtle poison that makes us sick over time.

If we are to live the Christian life, then we need to live it as God designed it to be lived. Don't worry—He isn't trying to shoehorn us all into uniformity. There's great latitude in His overall design for us still to be individuals. But we definitely need to get all the ingredients right. God makes it clear in His Word what's most important, and we are invited to follow the recipe to survive and thrive.

Hope for the Hungry

Before I became a Christian, I had a hard time believing that church people had something I would ever want to eat (using the previous analogy). The Christian life they exhibited did not seem to satisfy them in any visible way—at least as far as I could tell. Why would I ever want in on that meal?

Friends at school or work who were involved in different religions were just as happy—or unhappy—as many of my Christian friends, even though they followed a different path. I could detect few discernible differences. Some of the Christians I knew lived double lives. They had a "Sunday morning" language, kind and friendly and saying all the right things. Then they had an "at work or play" language—salty and full of criticism and complaining. I didn't expect them to be perfect, but they never seemed to look like they had found the answer to all their woes as they claimed. When honest, they would tell me they trusted few people and felt alone most of the time. They felt the pressure to be perfect in front of others, and only when they had a few drinks did the truth come out.

When I did see some Christians who were sincere about their faith, they just didn't seem to be joyful. The sky was falling because evil lurked everywhere. Others seemed to be almost overly joyful—almost delusional—as though it was wrong to admit something was broken in their lives because that would somehow make Jesus look bad. Most of these sincere believers seemed to be friendly, but they also didn't seem to have real relationships in which they could take down their walls. Either way, frankly, I didn't want to be around them.

Many were definitely "religious" in the sense that they lived with a list of dos and don'ts a mile long. But they seemed afraid of God and others rather than at peace the way the Scriptures promised. They'd often say that only through Jesus could a person be saved, but they didn't seem to be saved from anything the rest of us were dealing with in real life. Many who I thought were Christians didn't seem like they had any real desire to reach those of us who were "lost" either. If these Christians truly believed people were going to hell, then why didn't they share their faith—and do it with the social courtesies of gentleness and respect (1 Pet. 3:15)? Instead, there seemed to be an unspoken understanding among most believers I associated with that you kept your faith to yourself; you didn't talk about politics or religion—ever. I used to think maybe they were not very impressed with their faith because it really didn't change much for them, so why share it? Others were overly zealous and wouldn't quit talking about Jesus, but they didn't seem to understand that how they lived was being watched and had more power than what they said to us.

When I did attend a Sunday morning service, I noticed many of these same Christians called each other "brother" and "sister," but weren't they the ones who told me privately that they didn't really trust anyone? My dad was a pastor, and I'd see the stupid and trivial battles Christians fought with each other. Those battles didn't make me want to be involved in their so-called family. Again, there were always a few sincere Christians who were attractive to be around, but I saw too much of the other side—insincerity, game playing, bickering. I saw the constant struggle and brokenness of many, and I wondered what they got in this life for following Jesus. Sure, many talked about how their hope was in the next life and how that hope carried them through. They talked about forgiveness. They talked about grace. But there were a lot of gaps too. I couldn't discern any big benefit for following Jesus, particularly in this life. Christians were just as messed up as non-Christians. Something was definitely missing in the Christians' recipe for faith and life.

At the time I just thought the Christian religion was flawed at its core rather than misrepresented and misunderstood by its followers. Many years have passed, and I am now a senior pastor who has seen thousands of believers living out various forms of the faith. Every week in the church I lead, I see the good, the bad, and the ugly. I see committed Christians—those who definitely follow Jesus and rely upon the Word of God, the Spirit of God, and the people of God to help them mature in their faith. I get to see how God lives in and through them, and it's amazing. I also see casual Christians—those who show up every so often and call themselves "Christians," but their faith seems to be in name only, not in deed. They are playing a game, and no matter what Scripture says, they want to fit Jesus into a comfortable place in their lives. Sadly, they will never experience what Jesus has for them unless they choose to surrender to Him. I also see "religious" Christians who add to their faith long lists of rules. Their faith has become burdensome, and they are tired spiritually or, worse yet, they have become proud, deceived into believing they are worthy because they follow the rules better than others.

Either way, unfortunately they are not experiencing the life they could have in Christ because they have misunderstood or have, in reality, rejected the true faith. They may have much of the recipe for living powerful faith right, but they have missed a key component that affects their ability to fully experience what God wants to give them. This is often the result of a lack of biblical relational discipleship. They either never received it in the church they came from or they have rejected it because of past hurt or because it required too much change to their lives. Sadly, even in our church we have Christians who have heard about this component but have still missed the point. As I travel around the country to work with pastors and laypeople, I see the same problems. Plenty of Christians are alone and hurting, struggling to know what their faith is all about, desperately hoping for an experience in the Lord that's greater than what they currently have.

This book is for those who are missing something and are honest enough about that to look deeper—who truly want to follow Jesus no matter where He leads them. Even if it's uncomfortable and scary, it's when you trust Jesus to go wherever He leads that you truly experience a miracle. So many are close to tasting great lasagna, but it still escapes them. They're at church, hoping for truth, often committed to praying, knowing the Bible, worshiping God, and even evangelism, but still missing something important. The spiritual recipe they're cooking with doesn't satisfy—and they wonder what to do.

If that's you, then be encouraged, because hope is at hand. What I want to show you is the recipe for perfect lasagna. Sure, I know we live in a sin-soaked world and God doesn't promise us problem-free lives. I know the culture around us is polluted and there's a spiritual enemy who would love to destroy us. I know that in this world we will have trouble, because the Bible promises it (John 16:33). I know we all have a broken sin nature that fails to live out even the simplest recipe perfectly. But there is hope for those who become spiritually mature by feeding on God's spiritual food. We can have Real Life now that enables us to survive and thrive in spite of all we face. I know you want that as I do, so the question is this: What is missing from the recipe you have been living out? That is what this book is about.

Protecting the Recipe

One of my favorite passages of Scripture is Jude 3–4:

> Dear friends, although I was very eager to write to you about the salvation we share, I felt compelled to write and urge you to contend for the faith that was once for all entrusted to God's holy people. For certain individuals whose condemnation was written about long ago have secretly slipped in among you. They are ungodly people, who pervert the grace of our God into a license for immorality and deny Jesus Christ our only Sovereign and Lord.

Notice that Jude initially wanted to write an encouraging letter to the church. But there was a problem, so he felt compelled to write a letter of warning instead. The problem was that some people were perverting the message that had been handed down to them through the apostles, trying to change the recipe of faith. The word for "faith" here describes the body of knowledge—the right doctrine and lifestyle—that had been passed down from the apostles.

In Jude's specific case, the perverted teaching was that, because Christians are saved by grace, they can do whatever they want as it pertains to lifestyle. The false message was that Christians can even go on sinning although it hurts God and others. In this false recipe, grace was being turned into a license for immorality.

Jude was challenging the Christians to follow the right recipe, the recipe for faith that aligns the way we think and live with how God thinks and lives. Jude explained that this right faith recipe had been delivered once and for all, and that to change it was a big mistake—like sneaking poison into a product to sicken or kill those who consume it. Or to intentionally or unintentionally leave something out that would make the spiritual food powerful and effective. Jude is warning us that we have an enemy who seeks to monkey with our spiritual food.

The same is true today. Our spiritual food is susceptible to being poisoned by our spiritual enemy. The Bible warns us to hold on to the doctrine, teaching, and lifestyle modeled by Christ and the apostles. Paul says in 1 Timothy 4:16, "Watch your life and doctrine closely. Persevere in them, because if you do, you will save both yourself and your hearers."

That means we must "guard the recipe"—the faith—closely. Notice how Paul combines both "doctrine" and "life" in how we function as believers. It's easy for believers to forget to put in all the ingredients, but we must pay careful attention because God's intended recipe is perfect and must be followed and protected.

Here's my point: The faith handed down to us in the Bible is perfect, and the warning for messing with that faith is clear. When we consume the wrong recipe, it has dire effects on our ability to function correctly in the world we live in. The result is a malfunctioning faith that leaves people open to the kinds of things that destroy churches, families, and even eternities. Too many believers have been fooled into focusing on an incomplete recipe, and the result is that they lack the joy, peace, and strength that can get them through the battles they face. Some Christians have gone so far as to decide that because their faith (which is incomplete) isn't working, then perhaps Jesus isn't who He said He was.

Because so many Christians don't have a thriving Christian life, others falsely conclude there is no thriving spiritual life to be had. Still others have been shown a false Jesus (by His representatives), and they've rejected the faith outright. If those people could only see the real Jesus for who He is, then I believe they'd love Him. It's a sad state of affairs both for the surviving representatives (only barely surviving) and for those they could have helped if they had been eating the recipe Jesus intended them to be eating. (Okay, the Bible calls it "living bread," not Mom's lasagna.)

Sadly, when a human does not consume the right food, or enough food, or poisoned food, he does not have the strength to take on any great task. He doesn't have the ability to fight any significant battle for long because he is too weak; he just gets too tired. He does not have the ability to fight off sickness because his immune system doesn't work anymore. He needs healthy food, consistent food, and the right food if he is going to survive and thrive. The same principles apply in the spiritual world.

I'm intrigued by the survivalist-type shows on TV lately. I love the outdoors, so I find some of the information useful, but I also see great spiritual analogies in these shows. How easy it is for a starving person to become sick, because he's had no real nourishment for too long. In the same way, too many believers are living out a form of Christianity that is only partially correct. They have only partial effectiveness and partial defense against a spiritual enemy who longs to destroy them.

It happened just last week. A man I count as a friend informed me that he had cheated on his wife. He has been in church most every weekend for years. He knows his Bible. I've seen him pray. I've seen him worship and serve. He is in a powerful position in our community and has had a good effect for some time on both believers and nonbelievers.

What went wrong? He was trying to live on a faith recipe that left him open to spiritual attack. What did that look like? Whenever I asked him how life was going, he always said "fine." He insisted he was close to the Lord and in love with his wife and committed to his family. Whenever I asked him to join a home group and develop real relationships with other believers, he insisted he was "too busy for that kind of thing." Asked to define "busy," he rattled off a long list of activities: Sports for the kids. Family camping. Work, always work. The activities were fine in and of themselves, but when real relationship is a missing ingredient, then you have an incomplete recipe for a healthy spiritual life and disastrous results naturally follow.

This week, he needed to tell his wife the truth. Their relationship has a long way to go to be fully restored (hopefully it will be). Fortunately, he is back on track and willing to make time for what I asked him to do in the first place (really, the Bible *declares* he should do this). It would have been so much better if he had simply followed the complete recipe in the first place. It would have protected him from falling. Now he's following the recipe in a quest to salvage both a marriage and reputation that he very well may lose for good.

See, when God asks us to live our lives in a certain way, it's because He loves us. He knows how He designed us and what you and I need to survive and thrive. God hands us the recipe in the Bible, and if we leave one ingredient out, then the recipe will always come out second best. If we try to substitute more of one thing and leave out another, then the faith recipe will never be all it can be.

Just Me and Jesus Is Not Enough

My big goal for this book is to challenge what many believers think is the normal recipe for the faith. Many have heard and accepted the message that Jesus saves, but somehow missed that Jesus has something to say about how we live every day. Following Jesus in obedience is the very essence of discipleship. Sadly, far too many have not been discipled into maturity. They've either refused to become spiritually mature, or the person who initially shared the gospel with them did not invest in them to help them discover God's ingredients for a life-giving spiritual life. As a result, they are left with a hodgepodge recipe for the faith that leaves them wanting.

Many others are discipling other people because they see a need for spiritual maturity. But many in our culture are being handed an incomplete recipe for the life of faith. If those who would disciple others are missing something important, that gap is passed on to those they disciple. Most pastors and teachers have emphasized the need for understanding the Scriptures, and rightly so. You cannot be mature in Christ if you don't become familiar with God's voice through the Scriptures. However, I still believe something is missing. So what is it?

Did you know the entire Bible is about relationship? Not just relationship with God, but relationship with *other people* as well. The needful ingredient so many Christians are missing is the power that comes from being together.

The opening act in Scripture tells us we were created in the image of God. Later, both through Scripture and in the person of Jesus Christ, we learn that God is love. This means that we were created to be relational beings. God did not create us because He was lonely, but God is relational at

His very core. The Trinity—God the Father, God the Son, and God the Holy Spirit—has been in a love relationship for all eternity.

Consider the creation story in Genesis. God created one thing and then said it was good. He created something else, and again pronounced it good. That pattern was repeated until God created man and said something was "not good." And why? Because man was alone.

It's key to note that Adam wasn't completely alone. He had God, who walked and talked with him in the Garden. Imagine that—there was the first human enjoying a perfect relationship with his Creator, yet even then God said something was "not good." It's because Adam was created to be in relationship with other humans *as well as* with God. God created Eve so Adam could be in relationship with another human being.

Some might say God meant by this revealed scene that we all need a spouse. However, that interpretation does not jibe with Scripture. For instance, in the New Testament Paul reveals that for some it is better not to be married, just as he wasn't. No, what God meant is for us to have relationship with other humans, regardless of our marital status.

Many Christians today mistakenly believe the only thing that matters is their relationship with God. "It's just me and Jesus," they'll say. But that's not what Scripture tells us at all. We were created to love God and to love others. Both are important. Granted, your most important relationship is with God through Jesus Christ. It is out of the overflowing of an abiding relationship with Jesus that we have the capacity to be in relationship with others. But God tells us in His Word that to have real relationship with Him is to have real relationship with others.

Right away in Genesis, mankind found out what happens when we mess up relationships. The fall in the Garden of Eden was about people falling out of perfect relationship with God, resulting in death. Physical death, yes, but much more.

Our perfect relationship with the earth fell apart. Weeds began to grow to make life hard. From then on we'd have to work to produce food by the sweat of our brow.

The marital relationship was damaged. God told the woman that her desire would be for her husband but he would rule over her (Gen. 3:16). Every husband would like that to mean his wife would desire him physically (which would be great) while he gets to be boss! It actually means that the woman would desire to control her husband, but he would seek to rule over her, and a battle for control in the home ensued.

Relationships with children were supposed to be a beautiful thing, but instead there would be pain in childbearing (and those of us who have kids know there is pain in childrearing as well). Scripture reveals that there would be a spiritual battle from then on.

Ultimately, the death resulting from the fall was much more profound than we could have imagined—it was the death of right relationship. For beings created to be in relationship, this is devastating. The very thing we were created for and need would never be attainable because of sin, unless something miraculous happened to remedy the situation. That's a curse indeed.

In the midst of the Genesis story, an enemy is revealed and his intent is simple. If God is a God of relationship—then the devil's goal is to destroy relationship. The devil knew that to destroy relationship with God would be to topple the first domino in a potentially endless domino line leading to destruction. If relationship with God is lost then relationship between people also falls.

The good news is that God is a God of reconciliation and has orchestrated history to define His love, revealed as grace, giving us what we need rather than what we deserve. Jesus came into the picture to offer us the choice for restoration of all that had once been destroyed.

Jesus came to love and forgive us and restore our fellowship with God—and as a result, to restore our fellowship with others (1 John 1:7). The history of mankind began with perfect fellowship and will conclude with fellowship restored in a new heaven and a new earth. The Bible says over and over that God's desire is that we again will be His people and He will be our God. That's relationship!

As we unpack these ideas in this book, I want to make something very clear. There is a big difference between being friendly and polite to people and having real, life-giving relationship. I truly believe that most of our great biblical words have been stolen. Oh, we say words like *relationship*, *friendship*, and *love*, but these words have been redefined by our enemy, who often controls the culture, and they lose their power. It's up to us to look to Scripture as our guide for right definitions.

Yes, we need "relationship" with God and others. But it's very important that the "relationship" we seek is defined by Scripture, not the world.

Cheap Rafts on a Raging River

This past summer my wife, children, grandchildren, and I took a two-hour float trip down the beautiful Saint Joe River.

It is a slow-moving river where many a fly fisherman has found joy. Every summer people flock to the river with their rafts and tubes to take the leisurely, sun-filled trip. It's not unusual to see people and their tubes tied together in large numbers, with one tube dedicated to their radio, which is blasting (much to my frustration), and another tube dedicated to a cooler of adult beverages. Because the river is pretty shallow in the summer, few people wear life jackets. If it gets too bumpy, even youngsters can just stand up on their feet.

We didn't have enough tubes for everyone, so we picked up several cheap tubes from Walmart. Because the place in the river where we chose to float is so slow-moving, the eight-dollar tubes made it down the river with little problem. The sun was out, and our ten adults and two small children had a great time talking, splashing, and looking at the beautiful mountains as we floated by.

As I was floating down the river on a cheap, thin-skinned tube and no life jacket, a thought entered my mind: Would I float the river with my family on these same cheap tubes if this river was filled with class III, IV, and V rapids? My thoughts went immediately to no, and I asked myself, what kind of equipment would I require before taking this group down that kind of river? I pictured seriously expensive rafts with oars and life jackets. I pictured an alert and experienced river guide who'd been trained and knew the river's every turn. I pictured him training us to work together in the slow-moving water, getting us ready for what he knew was coming.

Then I thought about the Christian life. Too many Christians have a faith like an eight-dollar inner tube. Their tube might get them down an easy river okay, but if there is any kind of trouble or emergency or white water, then they'd be sunk. This kind of cheap faith will only support a person if the river of life leads along a slow, easy stretch of water. It's not a faith designed for serious rafting.

And here is the problem. The world in which we live today is not like the slow, leisurely river I floated on this summer. The river of life is designed for serious rafting. It's filled with rapids, increasingly dangerous and often at flood stage. Our culture has quickly moved to an anti-Christian position and most of us are not ready for it. If Christians are to survive this turbulent culture, then we will need a faith that is just as God designed it to be. God's form of Christianity is like that team of rafters with the right equipment, all working together to navigate dangerous waters.

My concern is that there's something missing, and the faith that most Christians have will not be enough. Christians are in for a very difficult time in the near future. Jesus made it clear that in the end times wickedness will run rampant, and the love of most will grow cold. Paul tells us false prophets and difficult times are coming—people will be lovers of themselves, lovers of pleasure, rash, conceited, and the like (2 Tim. 3:1–4). We are in those times now, and if Christians are to survive, they will need far more than an eight-dollar Walmart tube to take on a culture that is like a furious river without mercy.

When you go on a rafting trip, you discover in the slower water in between the rapids that you can tell when things are going to get hairy. You just listen for the roar coming around the next bend. Can you hear it? I sure can. What kind of tube are you on?

2

Hardwired to Connect

Have you considered that when God created us, He designed us all with a purpose in mind? Ephesians 2:10 tells us, "For we are God's handiwork, created in Christ Jesus to do good works, which God prepared in advance for us to do."

I love how the NLT puts it: "We are God's masterpiece. He has created us anew in Christ Jesus, so we can do the good things he planned for us long ago." This passage reveals that we were designed for an important purpose. Psalm 139:13 tells us we were knit together in our mother's womb for something important, and Ephesians 2 reconfirms for us that God knew us before time began. But often we read these kinds of passages apart from their context so we get the idea that Jesus doesn't care how and when we use these abilities. We can get the idea that the good works He prepared for us have little to do with the Lord's family here on earth.

You see, the Ephesians 2:10 passage concerning purpose leads us to Ephesians 2:19, where we are told we are a part of the Lord's family—the church. Later in Ephesians 4 we are told we are a part of the body of Christ and we are knit together, and God desires us to work together for His purpose and our maturity. We are told that we become mature as each part does its work together for the glory of God.

As individuals and as the corporate body of Christ, in relationship with one another, we are to commune with the Lord so that our good works can reflect His glory to a world badly in need of Him. The Westminster Shorter Catechism famously puts it this way: "Man's chief end is to glorify God, and to enjoy him forever." God's commands are given to protect His designed creation and especially the focus of His creation— humans. It means that when we live the way God intended, we can expect the best possible outcomes in our lives.

Jesus was once asked to describe what it means to live well in God's sight, although the question was worded a bit differently. Here's the context of Mark 12: Teachers of the law had gathered around Jesus as He taught in the temple courts for the express purpose of asking Him hard questions. Some of these questions were designed to trip Jesus up and discredit Him. One scribe asked Jesus whether they should all pay taxes to Caesar. But Jesus knew the hearts of the people around Him, and He understood the hypocrisy of the questioner. He asked to see a Roman coin and pointed out the image and inscription on it. "Give back to Caesar what is Caesar's," He brilliantly told them, "and to God what is God's" (Mark 12:17).

One question in the barrage of questions, however, was apparently sincere—and this question bears a closer examination. The scribe who asked it recognized that Jesus was a man who knew things, so he was sincerely seeking truth. His question pertained to what was most important in life. In that day, teachers of the law regularly discussed which commandments were most important. Traditionally, they had calculated that the Mosaic law held some 613 commandments. All were binding, yet they assumed some commandments were more significant than others. Here's how the conversation went down:

> And one of the scribes came up and heard them disputing with one another, and seeing that [Jesus] answered them well, asked him, "Which commandment is the most important of all?" Jesus answered, "The most important is, 'Hear, O Israel: The Lord our God, the Lord is one. And you shall love the Lord your God with all your heart and with all your soul and with all your mind and with all your strength.' The second is this: 'You shall love your neighbor as yourself.' There is no other commandment greater than these." And the scribe said to him, "You are right, Teacher. You have truly said that he is one, and there is no other besides him. And to love him with all the heart and with all the understanding and with all the strength, and to love one's neighbor as oneself, is much more than all whole burnt offerings and sacrifices." And when Jesus saw that [the scribe] answered wisely, [Jesus] said to him, "You are not far from the kingdom of God." (Mark 12:28–34 ESV)

It's interesting to me that Jesus was asked what the greatest commandment was, but rather than giving one, He gave the scribe two. Jesus told the man that love for God and love for others is highest on the Lord's priority list. Later He emphasized that "all the Law and the Prophets hang on these two commandments" (Matt. 22:40). Why would every law point to relationship, you might ask? Well, I believe it is because He knows exactly how He made us. I believe every command is for our good and His glory. You see, God designed us with relationships in mind—we are literally hardwired for relationship. It's a safe bet to conclude that when these relationships are in place, we are living as God intended. When we are living as God intended, it leads to a satisfying life. But if these relationships are not in place, our lives will be far less than He intended.

It's a lesson for modern times too. If we want to live well, as God designed, then our method for living must be God's method. We must focus on relationship, and our means to that end is to learn to love well. When this is in place, other qualities of life will follow.

Scripture teaches this in black and white. But did you know that secular studies also support this idea that we are hardwired for relationships? It's not that the secular studies somehow contain "more truth" than the Scriptures. It's that the secular studies undergird what the Bible already teaches.

For Want of Being Known

In his book *Anatomy of the Soul*, Curt Thompson, a psychiatrist, traces the surprising connections between neuroscience and spiritual practices.[1] Thompson is a Christian, yet he writes from a scientific perspective as well as a strictly biblical one.

He notes how science shows that when a person is honest and relates in conversation with affirming, interested listeners, the person's brain actually goes through a reconfiguration

1. Curt Thompson, *Anatomy of the Soul* (Carol Stream, IL: Salt River Publishing, 2010).

process where it is healed and made stronger. The brain of the person listening is equally affected in profound, positive ways. Thompson's big premise is that the more meaningful our relationships with others, the healthier our minds. Science has told us that we are not to be alone.

Thompson writes,

> For those who desire to follow Jesus, these findings in neuroscience reflect what we already know from Scripture—that God desires for our lives to be changed in concrete ways for the good of ourselves, our communities, and for humanity as a whole. He desires for us to tell a better life story than what we ever could plan for ourselves. By paying attention to how our brains and relationships shape each other, we create space for God to work. We create space to "be transformed by the renewing of [our minds], so that [we] may prove what the will of God is, that which is good and acceptable and perfect" (Rom. 12:2, NASB).
>
> Comprehending all of this begins and ends with understanding the difference between *knowing* and *being known*. *Knowing* is an activity of the mind that keeps the "knower" separated from the fact, idea, object or person/s he knows. Such separation is not so bad for facts, ideas or objects, but it is bad for people, who are meant to *be known* at a deeper level. *Being known* requires an availability, vulnerability, and trust of the person knowing you. It requires an understanding that there is no such thing as an isolated mind, and that life will only be full of joy, courage, kindness and security to the extent that one is engaged, known, and understood by another, especially by God.[2]

2. Curt Thompson, "Anatomy of the Soul," *Being Known*, http://www.being known.com/anatomy-of-the-soul/.

31

Another study bears close examination. This one is purely secular and found in a lengthy paper titled *Hardwired to Connect: The New Scientific Case for Authoritative Communities,* prepared by researchers at the Dartmouth Medical School Institute for American Values.[3]

To create their findings, a commission of thirty-three distinguished doctors, research scientists, mental health providers, and youth service professionals studied the rising rates of mental illness, behavioral problems, and emotional distress among American children and teens.

The commission came up with six key findings:

1. Humans are chemically predisposed to form close relationships.

When humans connect on deep levels with other humans, our brains see spikes of the attachment hormone oxytocin. This triggers senses of well-being and lessens feelings of aggression. Simply put, our biology works best when we form and sustain enduring, nurturing relationships with other people. We are hardwired to connect.

2. If a child experiences close, nurturing relationships while growing up, his or her brain is profoundly affected for the better. The opposite experience produces harm.

Nurturing and non-nurturing environments affect actual brain circuitry. When children grow up in secure, nurturing environments, their brains develop in ways

3. See Stephen J. Bavolek, ed., *Hardwired to Connect: The New Scientific Case for Authoritative Communities,* A Report to the Nation from the Commission on Children at Risk, Institute for American Values (with Dartmouth Medical School), Amp Publishing Group, 2003.

that help them have healthy relationships with others and help them better cope with stress. If these nurturing environments are not present, then a person's brain development is actually harmed and the person is more inclined toward depression, social isolation, anxiety, and other negative outcomes.

What can you do if you didn't grow up in a nurturing environment? See point number 3.

3. **Animal studies suggest that genetic vulnerabilities can be overturned by close contact.**

    In a long-term study undertaken by researchers at the National Institute of Child Health and Human Development, a large group of rhesus monkeys was divided into three subgroups, studied over several generations.

    In the first subgroup, the monkeys had a genetic vulnerability to anxiety and timidity.

    In the second subgroup, the monkeys had a genetic vulnerability to aggression and poor impulse control.

    The third subgroup was filled with highly nurturing monkeys.

    When the first and second subgroups were given access to negative environments, the effects were harmful. For example, when given unlimited access to alcohol, the monkeys drank heavily and steadily and often succumbed to early deaths.

    But when these first two subgroups were allowed regular interaction with the third subgroup—the nurturers—they thrived. Their anxiety, timidity, and aggression disappeared. They became monkeys that thrived.

4. **Teens and young adults particularly need healthy, nurturing, and close human contact.**

A person's brain goes through extensive rewiring through adolescence and into a person's early twenties. One chemical affected in a person's brain during those years is dopamine, the "reward" chemical. If a person is placed into nurturing environments where close, supportive relationships can be formed, then the brain does well. Conversely, if a person is immersed into non-nurturing environments where close relationships can't be formed, or where a brain is harmed by drugs, then damage is done.

5. **Humans are biologically primed to seek moral and spiritual meaning. Nurturing relationships are a central foundation for positive moral and spiritual development.**

Researchers found that humans are biologically primed to seek moral meaning and spiritual connection to the transcendent. This was a secular study, remember.

When humans connect deeply with others and with something beyond themselves, they develop altruism and empathy. Conversely, when these connections aren't made, humans develop antisocial behavior and low impulse control.

Simply put, it's built into our DNA to want to connect with God and others.

6. **Nurturing relationships and a spiritual connection to the transcendent significantly improve physical and emotional health.**

Dr. Stephen Bavolek, PhD, wrote a summary finding of this point:

As the foregoing evidence indicates, we are biologically primed to connect with other people and with moral and spiritual meaning and individuals who follow these biological cues are likely to be significantly healthier and happier than individuals who do not.

A large and growing body of research also demonstrates significant health benefits associated with religious faith and practice. For adults, religious practice correlates with improved overall health, increased longevity, higher levels of reported personal happiness, and a stronger sense of purpose in life. For adolescents, religious practice is significantly linked to higher self-esteem, more positive attitudes about life, reduced risk of intentional and unintentional injury, reduced substance abuse, and a range of other positive health outcomes.[4]

Once again, science confirms what Scripture has written from the very beginning.

Two Are Better Than One

My point is this: It makes total sense that a loving God commands us in Scripture to do things He knows we need to do. God designed us. We were created for relationship, yet because of sin we have lost our ability to experience relationship as intended. This leaves us longing for something, and left to ourselves we don't even know to seek it. We are broken without knowing what is really wrong. Even if we do realize we need love, without the Holy Spirit's guidance

4. Ibid., summary sheet, 4.

to understand what love really is and without His power to help us live it out, it becomes just a nice idea. Unfortunately, there are many lonely Christians who have misunderstood the Scriptures or have downright ignored so much of what they say. Many are committed to Christ, understand much of the doctrine in the Word of God, want to be moral, and might even share their faith with others, but won't experience all God has for them unless they are intentionally in relationship with other Christians. We can often short-circuit our ability to withstand pressure and to cope with anxiety and stress when we are not in relationship. We carry burdens we weren't meant to carry because we've created an incomplete form of Christianity. We fight the devil alone when this was not God's intention.

Without committed, intentional, loving relationships with other Christians, we are missing an essential ingredient of the faith. Worse, many Christian leaders don't understand the real problem, so they focus on an incomplete solution. Many pastors I connect with acknowledge that there are overwhelming problems in the church, but they don't see the missing ingredient in the spiritual lives of their people. Their goal is to give more information (I am not saying that this might not be a part of the problem) but don't understand that relationship is what helps people live out obedience—or understand how to practically discover and live out steps to change. Other pastors acknowledge that relationships are important and missing, but they have so many plates to spin that they cannot focus on a solution that makes sense. Because the modern church must appear a certain way, work a certain way, and people have grown accustomed to certain expectations, leaders exhaust themselves to preach better sermons, or infuse a church experience with better worship music, or build more comfortable and inviting buildings.

There's nothing wrong with better sermons or quality music or welcoming buildings, but the problem is so much bigger than any of those solutions can fix. The leaders are like doctors who see sick people and accurately identify symptoms but misdiagnose the cause, so they prescribe the wrong or incomplete antidotes. Many hurting people experience pain because they do not know God's Word and are hurting themselves, so yes, we should teach the Word. But the Word requires us to have relationships where it can be understood and applied. In relationship we find strength to live out the daily changes needed and explained in God's Word.

In a great book by Christian counselor Larry Crabb, he said that about 90 percent of the problems he encountered in his clients' lives could have been dealt with by a good friend, if only they'd had one. Instead, they were paying to see a counselor.

The goal for Christian leaders must be to design and lead churches where people are able to connect with other people and live out their faith through relationships. People need to know others and be known by others. God wants us to pursue honest relationships. God wants us to connect deeply with other Christians.

In Ecclesiastes 4:9, we find a powerful verse: "Two are better than one, because they have a good return for their labor." The context is that the writer of Ecclesiastes, probably King Solomon, had everything life could offer—money, fame, power. But though he had it all, he was miserable and depressed because he wasn't closely connected to others. (This sounds like most Americans, and even many Christians.)

'ocused on relationship, and without it, all
\sfy.

ge and others bring me to understand one of the
. s prime ways to destroy God's most prized creation—
humans. If God has revealed to us in Scripture the importance of relationship, then it makes sense that the devil works
strongly to destroy relationship. If God is a relational God
and He created us to be relational as well, then it makes
sense that the devil seeks to destroy relationship at every
turn within the Christian family. He hurts us by luring us
away from relationship with God, knowing the move pollutes
our capacity to be in relationship with each other. The devil
seeks to get us too busy for relationship with God and others. He seeks to get us to sin because sin by its very nature
destroys relationship—sin hurts God, ourselves, and others.
The solution is found in the Bible—God's revealed intent and
directions for salvation from hell and broken relationship.
In the Word we find the person of Jesus Christ, who modeled the perfect relationship with God and others and can
give us the power to walk toward what we were created for.

I'm aware of the arguments we toss up against having
close relationships. We've been hurt or disappointed. We're
wary of trusting others again. But we must take this risk and
pursue connection through all the obstacles. The devil knows
our support system collapses if he can keep us distracted or
separated. Yes, as an isolated Christian, you can still make
it to heaven. But while on earth, something will always be
missing. You will not experience all the good that God has
for you, and you will not be the light in the dark world that
God desires that you become. Sadly, when you disobey God
you are allowing the devil to win. When the devil tempts you

to sin it's because he is ultimately trying to steal from you, kill you, and destroy you. Of course, he won't tell you that. He will tell you sin is no big deal. But in the end, sin always makes you less than you were supposed to be and gives you less than you were supposed to get.

Not long ago I met with a major leader of a huge spiritual movement. This man and his family are the real deal and have been so for years. They love Jesus and are willing to risk in ways most of us cannot understand for the cause of Christ. God was reaching thousands through their ministry, and the numbers were mind boggling.

As we discussed their mission to make disciples rather than simply converts, I was excited about what I was hearing. This ministry had gone to great lengths to teach the truth to those they had won to Jesus. The team was excited about their progress, yet as we talked, I saw a tiredness in their eyes, a loneliness relationally on the team. The spiritual battle was taking a toll, and they had been hurt deeply by some they were working with. I asked them how much they were sharing with their people. After a few seconds of silence, one member spoke up; none of them had friends they could trust. They had all been hurt by others and had decided it was better to just go to the Lord about it.

At this point I asked God for His help in expressing my thoughts, and we began discussing what true disciple making is. It involves learning to be faithful, loyal, and trustworthy—developing characteristics of true spiritual friendship and love within the context of the spiritual family, the church.

The hard question then was, if those characteristics weren't present in those being discipled, were they truly making disciples? When we do our part to make disciples, it doesn't guarantee everyone will become what they should be, but at least some will grow to become great spiritual friends with whom we can be honest and vulnerable—those we can do life with. If we are truly making disciples like Jesus did, and we have the blueprint for maturity in the Scriptures, and we have the Holy Spirit residing in us, then our ministries should be producing the kind of people we can trust and love, as well as be loved by. Many who seek to make spiritual maturity the goal miss this essential relational truth in their understanding of discipleship.

As I'm writing this book, my family is going through a difficult time, and I'll be mentioning various stories from this season of our lives as the chapters progress. Right now my adult son, Christian, is at a treatment center for anxiety and depression. He is a Christian now and walking with the Lord and with fellow Christians in relationship, but in earlier years he was far from the Lord and was a drug addict. He went through two treatment programs and finally spent time in a homeless shelter. He eventually surrendered his life to Jesus and got sober. He is now married to a wonderful woman and has a brand-new child. While he was far from God, he had fathered another child, and once sober he took responsibility to be the father God wanted him to be. After several years of rebuilding, he became a youth minister. He did well in that role for some time. But in the last six months he has been struggling with anxiety in profound ways. A major part of the problem is that the damage done to his brain while on drugs has had a long-term effect. (Our past sin can leave lingering consequences that we must deal with even years later.) Currently, doctors are trying to regulate his medications, a process that can take a while.

Christian phones me every night from his treatment center. He's very honest with me, and he can't wait to share what he's been thinking throughout each day. Sometimes he feels trapped in lies that the enemy and his broken mind whisper in his ear. The conversation with me helps him get unstuck. For instance, the devil tries to tell him he's the only one to ever struggle like this. But as we talk things out, he realizes that he is not alone; many people (including me) have felt the way he feels. The other day, he felt so far away from God and unworthy. He doubted God because of his situation. As we talked through his honest doubts, I was able to go to Scripture with him and bolster his understanding of where God is even in times of darkness. Near where he is staying, he has a friend who visits him and together they speak about his struggles. This friend listens, cries with him, prays for him, and shares his own common struggles, and I can see Christian gain strength from his time with this man. Each time we talk, I can sense his head clearing.

This type of transparency is key for all of us, not only for my son. We need to be connected with other believers so we can share what we're struggling with, confess our doubts and sins, and pray for one another. So we can do life together. This is how God intended us to live, even through difficult times. I can't imagine what it would be like for my son not to have relationships built on honesty and support.

A Foundation of Relationships

Certainly we all have times in our lives when we need to be alone. Having time alone with the Lord isn't wrong. Far from it. This alone time can help us clear the cobwebs and reduce the noise in our lives so we can read Scripture and pray. But here's the thing about times of solitude. When those in Scripture were done spending time alone with God, it led them back to the people and the mission.

I think of the biblical examples of Moses on the mountainside, alone with the Lord; and David, alone in the early mornings, praying and writing in his prayer journal, which we call the book of Psalms. The prophet Elijah spent much time in solitude and prayer, but he also had a close relationship with Elisha, sharing his life and ministry as a mentor and friend.

John the Baptist, who may be the Bible's most famous recluse, also had friends he called disciples. When he was facing death because of his scrape with Herod, he shared his confusion and doubt with his friends, who then came to Jesus to ask if He was truly the Messiah (Matt. 11:2–3). This passage reveals that even prophets can struggle when life gets confusing. It also reveals how to deal with that struggle—you are honest with your friends and you seek Jesus.

Later, we again see the strength of the relationships John had developed. When he was killed, his disciples cared about him so much that they came and took his body from Herod the tetrarch and buried it (Matt. 14:12).

Over the years many have rightly pointed out that Jesus often withdrew to pray. They try to make the point that being alone isn't wrong, especially if you are an introvert. However, I often answer that view with a question. Scripture says Jesus withdrew to pray. Withdrew from whom? From the crowds and even the disciples is obviously the right answer. After He withdrew, what did He do next? He rejoined the disciples. You see, Jesus models the aspect of solitude and prayer and relationship. Jesus is characterized by relationship with God and with men, which makes sense when Scripture tells us the greatest commandments are to love God and others.

For us, an abundant life in Christ emerges when we put His Word into practice and build our house upon the rock of God's Word. An abundant life emerges when we take God's commandments about loving Him and loving others and we do exactly that.

The other day I heard a great example of what God can do when we are in relationship with Him and others. A young man I'll call Andy was pastored by a friend of mine. When Andy first came to my friend's church, he was timid, alone, all by himself. He was a Christian but young in his faith and very shy. He could hardly open his mouth to say something without blushing a deep shade of red. He definitely had a blossoming walk with God that was being nurtured through his reading of the Word and prayer. However, relationally he was awkward and distant. Because relationship was hard for him, he had come to the conclusion that it was okay for him to be a loner.

Now, the big blocks of my friend's church were in place: good biblical teaching. regular opportunities to worship the Lord corporately, service opportunities, and so on. But what Andy most needed was to connect with others. Because of a lack of relationship, he had misinterpreted some Scripture, and this was leading to pride and judgment in some situations as well as shame and guilt in others. He also had no idea how to apply some Scripture in practical ways, so his awkwardness relationally was accentuated. He had knowledge but little wisdom. Bottom line, he had accepted Christ but had not been discipled.

On one of Andy's first Sundays, my friend literally took him by the arm and introduced him around to other believers. They'd caught the vision and welcomed him warmly. Andy became part of a home group, and over the next months he began to blossom. At first Andy would say very little in the group. However, as time went on people would reassure him, which led to more confidence. When he was wrong about something, people were gracious and lovingly gave him some things to think about. He began to spend time with some he could form deeper relationships with and his fear of being known slowly faded. You see, those in the group gave him a living picture of how to deal with misunderstanding and how to talk about things in appropriate ways. Andy discovered he was not relationally inept; he just had not seen what relationship should look like before and he started to succeed rather than fail with other people. He discovered that the Spirit of God, the Word of God, and the people of God can help you to bear spiritual fruit like love, peace, patience, and so on. He would always be a quiet guy, but there was a depth about him that people didn't notice at first. In relationship, Andy began to flourish.

Today, several years after that first Sunday, Andy is married, and he and his wife have three beautiful children. As an elementary schoolteacher, Andy regularly impacts children's lives in a positive way. He's a church leader, discipling others and helping them grow as Jesus intended.

Together.

3

What Is Spiritual Maturity?

Some time ago a man started attending Real Life Ministries, the church where I am privileged to be lead pastor, and asked to meet with me. As we talked in my office, I gathered quickly that he was basically interviewing me to decide if he wanted to get involved in our church. He and his wife had attended for a few weeks, and the implication was that they would come to serve at Real Life if the meeting went well.

"I've discovered your problem," he announced. "You've got a bunch of immature believers who don't know God's Word. I can help with that."

His tone sounded sincere, but I wasn't signing on the dotted line just yet. "Out of curiosity," I asked, "how do you know this about our church after such a short time?"

"Well, I've sat in your services and watched the people who come here. I have also listened to your sermons," he said. "They're practical, but not nearly deep enough."

"Explain 'deep,'" I invited.

"A good sermon methodically and systematically unpacks every word of the text," he said. "It helps people gain knowledge of God's Word at the deepest levels. It goes to the Greek and Hebrew, and teaches church history as well." He paused, then added, "Your people need more Bible knowledge to make them spiritually mature."

I did not disagree with the need for deep understanding of the Word, but something was missing from his definition of maturity. Acting on a hunch, I asked him to talk about where he'd been to church and why he'd left to visit ours.

He shared his journey to faith. He had been saved at an evangelistic crusade and immediately been fascinated by the book of Revelation. A church in his town offered a series on the subject, so he began attending. The pastor there was known for his Bible knowledge, and his method for teaching was verse by verse. A robust biblical education was really important to that pastor, and he'd started an unaccredited Bible college that drew mostly from the surrounding community. The man speaking with me had committed himself to understanding the Word and stayed immersed in that knowledge-heavy environment for many years. While at that church, he had attended the in-house Bible college and countless Bible conferences, been to Israel on study tours, read everything he could get on doctrine, studied church history, and risen to the status of teacher in that church.

Two things caused him to move on. First, a church split had occurred when the senior pastor had been forced out. Second, his job forced the man to move, so he began to shop for a new church in our area.

It hadn't been easy. In the past five years, he and his wife had been to seven churches. The couple felt negative about them all for various reasons. He believed that God had given him the gift of teaching, and he tried to use that gift in every church he went to. Some churches would not allow him to teach because of his denominational background or because the teaching positions were already filled. When churches did allow him to teach, his time there never lasted long. If any of the leaders of the church didn't agree with his opinions, then the situation inevitably turned contentious. If not enough people attended his classes, then he blamed the leadership's lack of promotion and decided the people in that church didn't love the Word enough. I asked what the conflicts had looked like. He explained that in every case he believed he had been right, and those who disagreed with him either didn't have his level of education or the humility to listen and learn from him. I asked how the issues had been resolved. He made it clear that the only resolution he would ever consider was if the other party accepted his perspective.

Red flags went up in my mind, but I pressed on. I asked him what kinds of issues had been big enough to cause such strong separations. He gave me a list of what I consider secondary theological issues that have nothing to do with salvation (a major issue) and everything to do with styles of worship and various other church practices (minor issues). He felt that any unresolved disagreement indicated it was time to move on. There was never any serious effort at restoration, no working through things, no noble struggle to keep a relationship intact, no agreement to disagree on some issues . . . just *time to move on*. The couple had bounced from church to church to church, always with wreckage left behind.

Probing further, I asked if he had any deep relationships with other believers and, if so, to describe the relationships. I was fairly sure I already knew the answer.

"Well, I'm good friends with my wife," he said. "And I'm friends with Jesus." He also mentioned that he had some relationships with a few leaders he had known years before at his first church, but he admitted that he didn't talk to them much. He insisted that his relationship with his wife was all he really needed. I asked if he was accountable to anyone, and he stressed again that the Lord and his wife were sufficient.

By then I knew that he would not be a good fit in any leadership capacity in our church at the present time, but I wondered if he was willing to grow up and change. So I asked, "Have you attended any of our home groups yet? Have you gotten to know anybody who calls this church home?"

"No," he said. "I don't believe I need to do that, and I don't have a lot of time for those sorts of things."

That was my cue. It was time to stop probing and start sharing my conclusions. I told him I believed he may be a gifted teacher and that someday I would love to have him help us teach the Word to people. But before he could teach in our church, he needed to belong to a home group as a participant—not leading. I shared how I believe that mature people are able to be humble and submit to others even if the others don't have as much knowledge as they do. I explained that a group was important so he could prove he could love well and be in relationship with others. You see, I said, many Christians think they're spiritually mature because they know Bible stories and facts or understand correct doctrine. Some Christians even think they are mature because they follow rules or have the ability to teach. But if a person can't resolve issues or learn to work together in unity with other believers, or if he's not known for great love for others, then the Bible is clear that the person isn't truly spiritually mature. I told him we were very careful about who we established as a role model in our church (such as a person put in a teaching position), because what we elevate and celebrate people will aspire to become. I concluded, "If you prove that you're a great lover of God and of other people as well as knowledgeable, obedient, and a gifted teacher, then you'll show yourself to be a model to follow and we will let you teach."

Sadly, that didn't sit well with him. He believed his credentials should allow him to teach. He also believed he didn't have time for practical love and relationship with others. The man and his wife didn't come again. Last I heard, they've been through two more churches since our conversation. That man has accepted an improper definition of spiritual maturity rather than understanding God's definition. And it's only causing frustration, disappointment, and chaos in his life—not to mention the lives of others he's been teaching.

Adventures in Missing the Point

To be clear, I believe strongly that Christians need to know the Bible. Christians need correct doctrine. We need to obey God's directions for behavior and use the gifts God has given us. We teach those principles, and we stand firm on God's truth in our church.

Yet the Bible is also clear that Bible knowledge or even obedience to God's laws or using our spiritual gifts is not the complete definition for spiritual maturity. These things are important, but they're pieces of the bigger picture.

As I mentioned earlier, the entire Bible is about relationship. Remember, in Matthew 22:40 Jesus said that all the Law and the Prophets hang on loving God and loving others. Every law God gives expresses His desire to build and to protect relationships. Being spiritually mature means we understand the heart of God and seek to love what and whom He loves. It causes great difficulty for God's team (the church) when leaders miss the point. In many Christian circles, spiritual maturity has become about rule-following, gaining knowledge (which puffs up rather than builds up [1 Cor. 8:1]), and elevating highly skilled charismatic personalities. Then there are those who are left to themselves to discover what this maturity is and, in turn, develop a faulty version. They conclude that maturity is simply going to church and listening to a very intelligent person tell you what to believe; it's knowing the Bible; it's inviting friends to church to hear the gospel presented; it's being a greeter or usher or nursery worker. And the pinnacle is becoming a teacher like the person up front. Knowing Scripture and listening to good teachers are good, but these alone do not make a person spiritually mature or create a body of mature Christ-followers.

Discipleship includes not only knowing God and living a life of service to Him, but also developing the ability to share the faith as well. More than that, every believer is called on to learn how to help others become disciple-makers as well—maturing people helping others to mature. Our highest goal is to love God and to love others and to use whatever gift we have to show that love.

One of my favorite passages is found in 1 Peter 4:10: "Each of you should use whatever gift you have received to serve others, as faithful stewards of God's grace in its various forms." First, notice Peter is writing to Christians, telling us that we are each given gifts that we are to use for the Master. Note the word "serve" in the Greek is *diakonountes,* from which the word *deacon* is developed. We are all called to become like deacons—servants in the church. We are all called to minister to others as faithful stewards.

The word "steward" is key. In biblical times, a steward represented his master. The steward had no wealth of his own, but used his master's wealth according to the master's will and direction. The passage teaches that our job as believers is to use whatever specific gifts God has given as stewards or managers of what He has given to us. But we are stewards of what? We are to deliver the grace of God to others. The word there for "grace" is so important. It is a love that delivers unmerited favor. God wants to deliver love to others through us. Did you catch that? God is the great grace-giver for sure, but notice how He gives His grace. People in the church are His means for delivering His grace. For those who have a "me-and-Jesus-only" attitude, this should be a wake-up call. God desires to love us and be in relationship with us and that through us He will love others. His love flows to us, but we are not to be like a dam that merely blocks the love and creates a pool for us alone. We are to be like a river that allows that love to flow to us and through us.

To be mature is to understand the importance of a love relationship and to teach others that we miss something important outside of Christian relationship. This passage makes clear that we all have spiritual gifting, meant to be used for others. We get to help deliver God's grace to others—what a privilege. And through others, God delivers His grace to us.

The biblical goal of every believer is to make disciples who make other disciples—people who follow Jesus, are being transformed by the Holy Spirit, and join with Jesus and His people on His mission to restore relationship between God and mankind and between humans, one to another.

It's so important to fully understand what it means to be and make disciples. It's possible to disciple someone toward the wrong goal (or an incomplete goal) if we are not careful. Ultimately our goal is to produce accurate copies of Jesus. We must be making the kind of disciples that Jesus Himself produced.

Note the strong warning Jesus held forth in Matthew 23:15: "Woe to you, teachers of the law and Pharisees, you hypocrites! You travel over land and sea to win a single convert, and when you have succeeded, you make them twice as much a child of hell as you are." The Pharisees certainly put a lot of exertion into their disciple-making efforts. They would travel extensively to win even a single convert to the law of Moses as presented in Judaism. But then they prevented that convert from seeing the truth. The Pharisees taught a religious system that mandated rule-following and allegiance to tradition, rather than the pathway to freedom and life found ultimately in Jesus Christ. They were making disciples, but not the right kind of disciples. We need to take care not to do the same.

We see examples of this wrong sort of target practice in the modern church. Some believers are obedient in many areas, yet miss what's truly important. Some time ago in our town, a bunch of Christians stood on a street corner holding signs.

One man held a bullhorn. The signs were strongly worded warnings for unsaved people to turn away from the sins of "abortion and homosexuality." The man with the bullhorn was yelling loudly that the city needed to "repent or perish."

I couldn't see into these Christians' hearts. They might have been sincerely trying to obey God in holiness, evangelism, and service. But they missed the point by not expressing the heart of God toward all sinners. Where was the love? If God is a God of relationship, then how is relationship built by shouting at strangers? Where was the heart to care about the feelings of others? (What is gained by public humiliation for sin a person may not even know is sin?) Where were the gentleness and respect mandated by 1 Peter 3:15?

If these Christians wanted to carry signs, maybe their message should have been "God loves you and I love you too." Maybe in humility they could have shouted, "I am a sinner and it destroyed me, but Jesus has saved me and can save you too." Maybe they should have put the bullhorn away and tried to build genuine relationships with people—praying for them, caring for them, loving them to Jesus.

Love Never Fails

Again, if we want to disciple people toward true spiritual maturity, then we need to grasp the right definition of spiritual maturity as our target. For that, let's unpack 1 Corinthians 13. Paul describes a list of spiritual behaviors that the Corinthian church had obviously accepted as the most important.

According to this passage, Christians can have all sorts of gifts and abilities and do all sorts of wonderful things, but if we don't have love, then everything else is worthless. (Remember, Paul is being led by the Holy Spirit to reveal God's perspective.)

> If I speak in the tongues of men or of angels, but do not have love, I am only a resounding gong or a clanging cymbal. If I have the gift of prophecy and can fathom all mysteries and all knowledge, and if I have a faith that can move mountains, but do not have love, I am nothing. If I give all I possess to the poor and give over my body to hardship that I may boast, but do not have love, I gain nothing.
>
> Love is patient, love is kind. It does not envy, it does not boast, it is not proud. It does not dishonor others, it is not self-seeking, it is not easily angered, it keeps no record of wrongs. Love does not delight in evil but rejoices with the truth. It always protects, always trusts, always hopes, always perseveres.
>
> Love never fails. But where there are prophecies, they will cease; where there are tongues, they will be stilled; where there is knowledge, it will pass away. For we know in part and we prophesy in part, but when completeness comes, what is in part disappears. When I was a child, I talked like a child, I thought like a child, I reasoned like a child. When I became a man, I put the ways of childhood behind me. For now we see only a reflection as in a mirror; then we shall see face to face. Now I know in part; then I shall know fully, even as I am fully known.
>
> And now these three remain: faith, hope and love. But the greatest of these is love.

Paul's point is that while it's certainly not wicked to know the Word and be skilled in spiritual gifts, even with all this we can certainly miss what's truly important. If we're going to disciple people toward spiritual maturity, then we need to grasp the core practice and heart attitude of spiritual maturity.

Paul speaks with hyperbole in 1 Corinthians 13—a type of exaggeration that drives home a point. We can do some great things, he says, but without love those great things don't amount to anything. We can follow the rules, give away all our money, offer our bodies to the flame as martyrs, move mountains with our faith, fathom all knowledge and all mysteries, get doctorates in theology, and win every single game of Bible trivia ever invented. But without love, it's all for nothing.

Why did Paul, through the Holy Spirit's inspiration, give this strong directive to love? There must have been deep problems in the early church when it came to love. What sort of problems?

We know from 1 Corinthians 1:10–17 that the early church had a propensity to divide over its leaders. One Christian bragged that he followed Paul, another that he followed Apollos, and another argued that Cephas (Peter) was the one to follow. Still another Christian self-righteously argued that he followed Jesus and Jesus alone. First Corinthians 3:3 says jealousy and quarreling ran rampant in the early church. First Corinthians 4:18 indicates that some people had become "arrogant." Chapter 5 deals with a serious case of sexual misconduct, with a little "boasting," "malice," and "wickedness" thrown in for good measure. Chapter 6 describes Christians suing each other and dragging each other to court. Chapter 7 indicates that marriages were in trouble and singles were acting inappropriately with other singles. Chapter 8 says some believers exercised a great amount of spiritual freedom and lorded it over those who had weak consciences.

What could have solved all those problems?

Love!

With love, early Christians would have refrained from bragging about which leader they followed and valued Paul as much as Peter. With love, they would have respected each other's opinions and sought to put Jesus first. They would have graciously understood that all true believers follow Christ and that when it comes to influence of spiritual leaders, different people are drawn to different personalities and styles, but ultimately it's about Jesus.

With love, jealousy and quarreling would have been quelled in the early church. Christians would have known that Christ gives different gifts to different people, and they could appreciate and use their own gifts while also being grateful for the gifts of others. One Christian might be an amazing speaker. Another might excel in hospitality and be an exceptional host.

With love, arrogance would have been set aside. People would have considered others more important than themselves.

With love, Christians wouldn't have been suing other Christians. They would rather be wronged than hurt others or the Lord's reputation.

With love, marriages would have been strong.

With love, Christian singles would act appropriately with other singles. They would constantly treat others with discretion and honor, and consistently want the best for others.

With love, Christians with much spiritual freedom would have been sensitive to Christians with weaker consciences and avoided offending them. The stronger believers could easily abstain from things that distracted from Jesus.

Love was the solution! It was the solution then in the early church, and it's the solution now in the modern church. If we don't have love, then we might have acts of service and evangelism and knowledge and hospitality and great teachers and awesome worship experiences and the best youth ministry programs ever, but we've missed the point. If we are to be spiritually mature, then we must be able to supernaturally love!

Some might accuse me of focusing too much on one passage. But the idea of loving others as a sign of spiritual maturity is found throughout the Bible. For instance, in 1 Corinthians 3:1–3, Paul says,

> Brothers and sisters, I could not address you as people who live by the Spirit but as people who are still worldly—mere infants in Christ. I gave you milk, not solid food, for you were not yet ready for it. Indeed, you are still not ready. You are still worldly. For since there is jealousy and quarreling among you, are you not worldly? Are you not acting like mere humans?

Notice what marked the Corinthians as immature infants in the faith. It was not their knowledge of the Word. Paul would later tell them that they had great teachers. It was not lack of skills and gifts. Paul would affirm their many gifts later in the same letter. What marked the Corinthians' immaturity was lack of love. Paul chastised them for quarreling and jealousy. Spiritual maturity was tied directly to their ability to be in relationship with one another.

Paul again deals with the issue of maturity in Galatians. He reveals to believers what a Holy Spirit–filled person looks like in Galatians 5:22 and following. As we increasingly yield ourselves to the power and presence of the Holy Spirit, He helps us set aside the desires of the flesh and walk in step with Him. The results are known as "fruit." "The fruit of the Spirit is love, joy, peace, forbearance, kindness, goodness, faithfulness, gentleness and self-control. Against such things there is no law" (Gal. 5:22–23).

All of the fruit points toward our ability to be in relationship as believers. Speaking to the body of believers in Galatia, Paul shares that if the Holy Spirit is working in the body, there will be joy. Yes, personal joy for sure as we look at Christ, what He has done, and what He promises for the future, but also collective joy as we do life together. When the Holy Spirit fills our lives with joy, we are more pleasant to be around. Paul tells us that one fruit of the Spirit is peace—yes, internal peace that passes all understanding, but peace in the body of Christ too. There is a lack of conflict because we look past faults and give grace. When contention arises, we handle it in a way that brings a sense of resolution and peace.

All of the fruit of the Holy Spirit are others-related.

We are kind *to other people.*

We are good and patient toward *other people.*

We are faithful to the Lord in our dealings *with other people.*

We are gentle *with other people.*

We exhibit self-control *around other people.*

We are all called to grow up in the faith, and that means we become more relational, because God's Spirit lives inside of us. To become mature in Christ means we use our abilities to serve others. Yes, we have gifts that are needed, like the gifts of teaching or knowledge. But love and the resulting relationship is the essential proof that we have become mature. Paul makes it clear that every gift given was for the edification of others—to build up the body of Christ. When people humbly use their gifts to minister to others, it develops strong ties that bind us together in relationship and furthers the mission of Christ.

Beyond Surface Politeness

True spiritual maturity must be every believer's goal. Paul laid out the target for us explicitly in Galatians 5:6: "For in Christ Jesus neither circumcision nor uncircumcision has any value. The only thing that counts is faith expressing itself through love."

Paul was trying to head off the misguided idea that was beginning to infiltrate the early church. Christians were tempted to make the mistake that Jewish teachers had made in Old Testament times. Remember that Abraham was credited with righteousness because of his faith. True faith—trusting God's promises—has always been what saves. But rather than trusting and obeying God because He is God, the Jewish leaders had started to think that following God perfectly would save them. You see the difference? On one pathway we trust in God, and on the other pathway, in ourselves. The Jewish leaders' rule-following became the faulty means whereby they hoped to gain salvation. This rule-following became a competition and source of pride rather than a pathway to God.

The Bible is clear that if we approach God by trying to be perfect in our own strength and righteousness, we will fail, because none of us can do the right thing perfectly every single time for the right reason. Jesus told the Jews that to hate your brother was the same as killing him in God's view (Matt. 5:21–22). Or to lust for a woman was the same as adultery (Matt. 5:27–28).

Trying to approach God based on our righteousness alone always leads to despair, because we discover we are not righteous by God's standard and cannot be. Some people are fooled into watering down true righteousness and become proud when they compare themselves to others rather than to God's standard. Pride separates us from God because it does not leave us humble enough to receive what we need. Pride destroys relationship with others, because if our status depends on our success and we realize we are failing, then we hide and separate from others.

If we are fooled into believing we measure up on our own, then we will believe others should too, and we will judge them. Again, this destroys relationship. The Jewish leaders had missed the point that none of us can perfectly follow the rules that were supposed to protect relationships perfectly. Romans 3:20 says, "Therefore no one will be declared righteous in God's sight by the works of the law; rather, through the law we become conscious of our sin."

The solution is that we all need a Sin Bearer. We need Jesus. Only Jesus has perfectly fulfilled the law. The Jews had strained out the gnat and swallowed the camel—and now the early Christians were on their way to doing the same. They were completely missing the point.

Paul called the line of thinking that espoused rule-keeping a "yoke of slavery" (Gal. 5:1). Then came the bottom line for Paul: "The only thing that counts is faith expressing itself through love" (Gal. 5:6). Those are strong words. Look at them again. Faith must be expressed through love. It's *"the only thing that counts."* Real faith leads to humility and thankfulness before God as we accept His solution for our sin problem. Real faith in Christ leads to an understanding of God's heart to restore relationship with Him and with others. Real faith gives us the Holy Spirit, who begins to change our hearts toward others. God's heart is to save and to rebuild. As we grow up we begin to love what He loves—ourselves and others.

I was privileged to know the legendary Avery Willis, a prominent leader in the Southern Baptist Convention, who passed away in 2010. We became fast friends and shared a heart for real discipleship in the American church. After reviewing some of our training here at Real Life Ministries, Avery became passionate about us partnering with key leaders in his group of churches. Avery invited me and a few leaders from my church to do a presentation to leaders from his convention. Our method for training at our seminars is to limit the up-front talking. We put people into groups with leaders and help group members experience a relational environment for discipleship.

I spoke about discipleship and the need for real relationships as the best method for making disciples, and then posed questions for the groups to discuss. Avery was in a group with some key leaders. After several minutes, Avery called me over to his group to answer some questions. In front of the men and women in his group he posed a question (he knew exactly what he was doing): "Jim, you keep talking about relationships. What does that look like in a church staff? It seems so fundamental a concept to you, yet I wonder if you could help us all better understand the practical outworking of that word—*relationship*—particularly in the context of church organization and management."

"Sure," I said. "If we're on the same staff together, then it means we are honest with one another about our walks with God, our families, marriages, and struggles with sin. When there is conflict in our relationships with others (and there always will be), we are lovingly honest and deal with the conflict quickly as Scripture tells us to. There is mutual accountability to be followers of Jesus, enabling us to be confronted in love as bosses as well as giving us the mandate to share our struggles with others. Christianity supersedes organizational structure. As staff members, we are brothers and sisters who walk the same road together. We pray for each other. We support each other. We don't put up façades. We're real with each other. We wash each other's feet, so to speak. We spur one another on. We sharpen one another as iron sharpens iron. We give cups of cool water to each other in Jesus's name. We work relationally together. We're on the same side. Essentially, we model the relationships we expect others to have with their families, friends, and co-workers."

After I finished there was silence for a minute. Then one of the leaders said, "Jim, that's quite interesting. But let me be really honest with you. I think we are going to struggle with that within our denominational churches for several reasons. We have had a tendency to replace the word *love* with politeness. We're friendly, but we can also be very guarded. We often don't trust each other with the deeper things of life because we fear for our reputations. We're nervous. That sort of stuff might be used against us later. As it pertains to the boss-employee relationship, this will be a struggle as well. We tend to have the mind-set that pastors hold people accountable, and so our pastors may feel it's disrespectful if a staff person confronts or corrects them. I believe staff pastors under a senior pastor would be very hesitant to do that, fearing repercussions."

As he spoke, I knew he was willing to say what so many others wouldn't—he was being honest, and he was correctly identifying the problem not only in his denomination but in most. As I and my staff have trained churches all around the world, we have discovered that indeed the church has become adept at being polite and friendly. Christians keep their true feelings underground. They don't confront issues, and there is little mutual trust or accountability. But there is a huge difference between being friendly and being in relationship.

True relationship is different from surface politeness—it goes much deeper, and it's life affirming. As believers, many of us hesitate with this idea of "relationships." We replace true love with civility. It makes sense that people in a church will live this way if the leaders have settled for it. We have a saying in our church: Where the head leads the body follows. Politeness is a cheap imitation of the needed thing, and it will not satisfy the relational need within us all.

The Hard Work of Real Love

If we think loving others is easy, or if we have an oversimplified idea of the practical outworking of the gospel, then we don't have much experience yet with loving others. Loving others is hard work. That's why Paul pointed so strongly to the need for love in every book he wrote to Christians. If it wasn't a daily choice and a constant struggle, then why would he have to write about it to Christians every chance he got?

Too often pastors try to discover some "new truth" in Scripture so they can give their people a different, exciting view of an old told truth. They know people have heard the basic Bible stories and applications many times, and they don't want people to be bored, so they search high and low for some way to "wow" their people. But I contend there is another way to keep people from being bored—teach them the simple truth that they need to love others in relationship, and then let them at it. It's messy, sure, but there is nothing boring or easy about it.

In our church several years ago, we had a brand-new couple accept Christ in a weekend service. It was great, but we knew they would need to be part of a spiritual family (home group) so they could grow up in Christ. Our home groups are where our more mature believers pour into the lives of our people. This new couple accepted the invitation to get involved in a home group, and the real work began. The group's job was to help them understand what it means to love God and love others.

The couple's lifestyle had led them into a mess, which was why they wanted to be saved in the first place. The answer to their overall problems was not simply to get baptized and start coming to church. They also needed help to untangle their lives and sort out the mess they had created by doing things their way for so many years. We knew that since God had led them to salvation, He also desired to lead them to spiritual maturity. They were to become disciples who would someday make disciples themselves.

Until then, they had a family who would model and teach so they could see the difference between what they had and what they needed.

Sometimes new Christians demonstrate quick and miraculous spiritual maturity in one area or another, but every one of them needs spiritual relationships centered around discipleship. For some, an addiction to alcohol disappears overnight. But usually God allows sanctification to work out in people's lives more slowly and with the help of others. Jesus saves people instantly, yes. He transitions their lives instantly from spiritually dead to spiritually alive. And we are instantly declared righteous because of Jesus's work on the cross for us. But practical holiness develops over time.

This particular couple had struggled in their marriage for years. After several affairs, they were on the verge of divorce. The husband was knee-deep in pornography, and the wife was spending too much time on Facebook with a man she called "just a friend."

As the group spent time together, the people were honest with their own struggles. At times the men would meet upstairs and the women downstairs, reading Scripture, praying, and sharing each other's struggles and successes. As time went on, the woman started to open up and share her frustrations with her husband in the women's group. At first she sought to justify what she was doing and expected them to agree with the direction she was going. When she had shared with unsaved friends, they would sympathize and agree that she deserved better. They would tell her there was nothing wrong with being close friends and emotionally intimate with another man. But the women in her home group gently led her to understand what Jesus wanted from her.

As time went on, she began to change from the inside out. This led to a confession to her husband and an end to the Facebook relationship. I would like to say that this led to an immediate end to their problems, but life is messy and growth takes time. I would like to say that if you do the right thing, it will lead to life as you want it. This wasn't the truth about this situation. For a while, the couple separated, and the home group members housed the husband while they worked through the situation. The group kept loving and supporting this couple, all the while praying with them, listening to them, and spending time with them. The good news is that they're still working through issues, growing up in their faith, learning how to truly love God and others—and they're doing it within a healthy community of people who love and care for them.

That's what discipleship looks like—learning to love in real relationships.

We Walk the Road Together

Jesus doesn't call us to comfort, to avoidance of hard things. He asks us to take up our cross and follow Him, even when it's uncomfortable. When Jesus asked us to carry a cross, it wasn't a beautiful gold cross hanging around our necks. It was a method of torture. This means that Jesus was asking us to deny ourselves and be willing to live for Him no matter what. As this pertains to relationships for believers, it means that we fight for resolution even when it's easier to blame others or withdraw in self-protection. It means we trust again when we have been hurt. Many people are willing to receive the good things of faith but not willing to suffer through trials. If God is a relational God and we were created to be in relationship, and if relationship (loving God and others) is His highest priority, then it's time we put it at the top of our priority list too.

What I advocate is establishing a way of doing life together. To stop holding each other at arm's length. It's about baring our soul in stages: Baring a lot to a small select group of close friends, the way Jesus bared His soul to Peter, James, and John; then sharing slightly less to a larger group, as Jesus revealed Himself to the Twelve; then baring slightly less to our largest groups, such as a congregation. In other words, I am not saying we share everything with everyone, but we do share with some. It means that the tone of our lives is one of love rather than pretention and isolation.

I advocate that all of us as believers stop thinking of church as somewhere we go for only one hour a week. We want everything in an hour these days, but that can't happen. If we want to become truly spiritually mature, then we must accept that everything we need—all the fellowship, encouragement, transparency, teaching, worship—won't all happen in a building one hour of one day in a week.

The key is to work toward real relationships, not just do the small group program. Do real life together. Call and text each other during the week. Eat at each other's homes. Pray for each other regularly. Talk openly and honestly with each other. A home group is the next step for those who attend a worship service, but there is more to it than that. The group becomes the launching pad to the next step—doing life with others. Jesus said, "By this everyone will know that you are my disciples, if you love one another" (John 13:35).

Learn to love.

That's the key to true spiritual maturity.

4

The Gospel of Relationship

The bottom line for spiritual maturity is love, according to
1 Corinthians 13. But what is real love? Have you noticed that
almost every song on the radio is about love? Most movies
on the big screen offers some kind of primary or secondary
romantic plotline. Most TV shows portray a love interest.
Most novels—thriller, mystery, or contemporary romance—
weave a love story into the mix. Most Country & Western
songs seem to be about a love found or lost (usually lost,
along with the house, horse, boat, and dog). Our culture
is infatuated with real love. Why? Because we know down
deep that we need it.

As Christians, we've seen that the devil loves to play word
games. Taking many of our key words, like *love,* he changes
their definitions. When we let him do this, these words lose
their power. I can think of all kinds of ways the enemy has
done this in our culture—even in church culture. *Worship*

has become about music that creates feelings rather than about surrender and praise to God. *Leadership* has become about dictatorship or politics or giving people what they want rather than what God says they need. *The church* has become a building rather than a body of believers. And *love* has become a feeling.

Typically, even in the church, when people say they love something, they mean they feel fondness for a person, place, or thing that makes them happy. They get a strong feeling of longing or excitement. They love something because there's big perceived benefit. They love another person because that person is kind, funny, or treats them well—ultimately makes them feel good about themselves.

But is that all love is? What if you love somebody and he lets you down? Or a person stops being all you hoped she would be? Or a person never lives up to your expectations? What then?

For Better, for Worse?

The answer from many Christians, unfortunately, does not sound much different from the answer of non-Christians. When the feelings die, they tell me something like, "I just don't love him anymore." Or "I love her, but I am not in love with her." They relish telling me God wants them to be happy and love just shouldn't be that hard, so they are moving on to find their true soul mate.

Paul closes the loop on the subject of love in 1 Corinthians 13. Remember, he made it clear that maturity is more than knowing the Word, more than understanding the mysteries of faith, more than the giftings of preaching or speaking in tongues of angels or men. It's even more than a commitment to Christ that may lead to martyrdom. Without love it all means little. But notice the direction Paul takes next. He defines love. Why? Because the definition had been stolen by the enemy. The world has corrupted love—our most important ingredient for relationship. Paul defines and describes the real thing in 1 Corinthians 13:4–7:

> Love is patient, love is kind. It does not envy, it does not boast, it is not proud. It does not dishonor others, it is not self-seeking, it is not easily angered, it keeps no record of wrongs. Love does not delight in evil but rejoices with the truth. It always protects, always trusts, always hopes, always perseveres.

Notice he tells us that love *is* something, and there's no mention that love is a *feeling*. Now, I am not saying love does not come with feelings at times, but to limit love to a feeling is a big mistake biblically. Real love as God defines it is a choice that leads to actions described in the Corinthians passage. For the most part, we Christians have done a good job at understanding this kind of biblically defined love when we think about God's love toward us. John 3:16 starts out, "God so loved the world that he gave." Romans 5 talks about how God loved us even while we were enemies (vv. 6–11). We can see that God is love and He asks us to love like He loves. *Agapaō* is a benevolent love—the kind of love that is filled with mercy and forgiveness. God's love is a grace-giving love that looks past our faults when we are in Christ. I am so glad that our God continues to pour grace into our lives as I constantly struggle to be all He saved me to be. He did not give me a one-time deposit of grace but keeps pouring into my life.

Some in the faith have done a good job of teaching that we are to love others in the same way God loves us. Christian love must be *agapao* love—a wildly selfless, unconditional sort of love that Jesus modeled for us when He laid down His life. As an act of the will, we give other people what they need rather than what they deserve. We love people regardless of their lovability; we love people because Jesus commanded us to love people. This is good and God-honoring, and definitely part of what it means to follow Jesus.

Recently I met with a couple who had tried out a dozen different churches in our area and even had been members of some for many years before coming to us. They weren't happy with any of the churches nor particularly happy with us either. But at least they were willing to come and talk about it. I discovered that they had been married for more than fifty years, which is commendable. So I asked them, "As spouses, have you ever disagreed with each other over the course of your marriage?"

They both nodded and said, "Sure."

I continued. "What did you do then, when you disagreed with each other?"

"Well," said the husband, "we prayed for each other, and we talked it out." He said he had to go to Scripture over and over again at times to wash the world's way of doing things out of his mind. The wife agreed. As they talked about how to make a marriage work, they shared both frustrating times and peaceful times that resulted from sticking it out, all the while quoting portions of 1 Corinthians 13 that had helped them define what God wanted in a marriage. I asked what issues they had begun disagreeing on and how they ended up coming to their resolutions. I asked them if they still had to accept things about each other after all these years that they wish they could have changed. Of course the answer was a humorous yes as they looked at each other.

I asked a follow-up question. "In the midst of any of your disagreements, did you ever wonder if the grass was greener elsewhere? Were you ever tempted to leave your spouse for someone else?"

They both chuckled. The wife answered first. "I would never let my mind go there. I was committed to him for life."

The husband said, "We came to understand that the grass is never truly greener. It only sometimes looks that way. But every husband and wife disagree sometimes, same as us. We knew we loved each other for better or worse."

"So let me ask you a final question," I said. "You've applied biblical truth and principles about marriage to your lives so well. You have talked about forgiveness and confronting and looking past issues. But you know that the Scriptures give us so much about how to act in the family of God too. So why haven't you applied Scripture to your dealings with people in your spiritual family at church the way you have in your marriage?"

They both silently looked at me and let the question sink in. I encouraged them to read together through Ephesians 4–5. Chapter 4 deals with unity and maturity in the body of Christ. Chapter 5 compares this picture to marriage. In fact, this powerful verse, Ephesians 5:21, "Submit to one another out of reverence for Christ," comes in the overall foundational context of Ephesians 4:3, "Make every effort to keep the unity of the Spirit through the bond of peace." As spouses, we want to be committed to each other for better or worse. As Christians, we need the same level of commitment to our church families.

You see, many like to use the Scriptures meant for the church context only for the marriage context, and I think this is a huge mistake. First Corinthians 13, which is read at many marriage ceremonies and may be important for marriage, is about the church according to the writer—Paul, inspired by the Holy Spirit. Often we forget that relationship in the church is to be so close that it can be termed *family*. So many people who are deemed mature fail to have the kind of relationships described here with anyone other than their spouse and thus completely miss the intent of these passages. We are called to weave the 1 Corinthians 13 kind of love into our relationships with other believers.

A woman in our home group recently described to us how she continually takes 1 Corinthians 13 and puts our names and faces behind each directive, asking herself questions along the way. *Am I being patient with Jim? Am I being kind to Jim?*

That's exactly what we all need to do with those we are called to love. Are we truly loving people the way Jesus wants us to love?

The Connection between Love and Relationship

Here's where the total love package can get tricky, and I invite you to closely follow this train of thought: There's a distinction between "love" and "relationship." They're not the same, either in concept or in practice.

Jesus wants us to love everyone. He also wants us to be in relationship with others. Sometimes Christians mistakenly think that if we simply love people through our actions (like being polite, kind, and generous), then we are relational people, but that's not necessarily the case. We need to move beyond loving everyone at arm's length, so to speak, to being people in relationship—even if that's hard. Our call is to "do life" with others, and as we journey the road together, we not only learn to love others, but we allow them to really know and love us too. When I say a person needs to be known, I mean they need others to know their real struggles and potential weaknesses that can be exploited by the enemy. It means they have people they can be honest with when they are struggling. We all struggle in many ways, and our inner world of the thought life is where the battle is won or lost. This battle is not to be fought alone.

As I traveled to my favorite hunting spot recently, I listened to a well-known pastor on the radio. He was preaching through Deuteronomy and came to the passage that declares that the people of Israel would be judged because they were not worshiping with joyful hearts. His application to this was to challenge those who whine too much. He referenced a new movement that teaches people to be honest with their struggles. He countered this by saying we are to take captive every thought and not voice the struggle because it gives it more power in your life. It seemed to me that he was shaming his listeners for ever feeling downcast, and insisted that Christians only be filled with joy. He seemed to be chiding people who were "dumping negativity" on others. He also stated he didn't want to hear it anyway, and people should just grow up.

I was shocked and concerned about what his listeners were hearing. My thoughts went immediately to Romans 12:15, where Paul tells us to "mourn with those who mourn." How can we do that if no one will speak the truth about what's happening in his or her life? Galatians 6:2 tells us to carry one another's burdens. How can we do that if we don't know who is laboring under heavy burdens? What about people dealing with clinical depression? Or with genuine doubts? How can I ever snatch a person from the fire (Jude 23) if I don't know he's in trouble?

The truth is, we need a group of people who can journey the *real* road of life with us. We need to both love these people and be in relationship with them, for this gets at the heart of love's totality. We need to love others, and we also need to let them love us back, as God's Word makes it clear that His answer to prayer for strength often comes through other believers. That's what relationship is about.

First Corinthians 13 tells us that love "always trusts." Trusts who? Paul is speaking about real love relationships with other believers. He says love trusts others even when you don't feel like sharing. The devil will definitely speak into your mind that you can't trust others, that they will look down on you for your struggles. That they will judge you and maybe gossip about you. The devil will shame you into thinking you are a failure, and that you are the only one who struggles. But when we trust others, we find that we are not the only ones who have a battle going on between our ears. When we bring our internal battle into the light, we find grace—God speaks grace into our lives through others. The gift of mercy is given to us through real friends. The gift of wisdom is given because another can see the forest for the trees when we cannot. Chains are broken and strongholds are destroyed when we have real relationship.

Leading in Loving Relationships

Jesus's primary purpose for coming was to die for our sins. Jesus has also given us an effective and reproducible model of discipleship we can follow as we walk through the gospel story. Regarding spiritual maturity in Christ, He gave us a perfect picture of faith walking itself out through love, a picture that we can emulate. We see what relationship is supposed to look like when we see Jesus interacting with others throughout the Gospels. It had such a profound effect on the disciples that they often, later on in Scripture, unpacked what they saw (or heard about from the other apostles who had seen something unique in a different encounter). For instance, look at Paul's writings about the way Jesus lived.

> Therefore if you have any encouragement from being united with Christ, if any comfort from his love, if any common sharing in the Spirit, if any tenderness and compassion, then make my joy complete by being like-minded, having the same love, being one in spirit and of one mind. Do nothing out of selfish ambition or vain conceit. Rather, in humility value others above yourselves, not looking to your own interests but each of you to the interests of the others.
>
> In your relationships with one another, have the same mindset as Christ Jesus: Who, being in very nature God, did not consider equality with God something to be used to his own advantage; rather, he made himself nothing by taking the very nature of a servant, being made in human likeness. And being found in appearance as a man, he humbled

himself by becoming obedient to death—even death on a cross! (Phil. 2:1–8)

This paints a complete picture of love for us. Jesus loved sacrificially. He gave what was needed at the expense of His whole person. As believers, with the Holy Spirit's help, we can grow in this kind of love as well. Paul writes later in this same letter that we have Someone inside who enables us to both will and to do His good work. So the challenge here from Paul is to let Him do it.

Thanks to the Holy Spirit, we now have the ability to love—if we choose to let Him work in us and follow the Scripture's leading. The Spirit gives us the ability to interact with other people without being conceited or selfish. We can have the relationship that the Son had to the Father—listening and then obeying. Jesus, even though He was God, allowed Himself to be wrapped in human flesh. He took on the form and likeness of a human being. He interacted with the Father in humility, not in arrogance, although Scripture tells us that Jesus was equal to God. We see this amazing relationship being modeled all through the Gospels.

The disciples were consistently difficult to love, yet Jesus loved them anyway. Once, the disciples were in the midst of a storm, trying to row across the Sea of Galilee to safety (Mark 4:35–41). Jesus was asleep in the stern of the boat. They woke Him up and accused Him of not caring for them. Jesus got up, rebuked the wind and waves, and the sea became calm. Then we find this amazing exhortation of Jesus to His disciples: "Why are you so afraid? Do you still have no faith?" (Mark 4:40). Here's the example for us to follow: When the disciples didn't trust Jesus, He still cared for them.

Although they did not trust Him and continually lacked faith, Jesus still revealed Himself to them rather than withdrew. He pressed into relationship, and His continued faithfulness to them, in spite of their failure, reveals much to us about what real love looks like.

But Jesus did more than just model love for difficult people. He modeled relationship with them. He not only loved others, He allowed others to love Him too. He not only knew others, He allowed Himself to be known by people.

One of the most profound passages in Scripture is Matthew 26:36–42. It's the night Jesus will be betrayed by Judas. Jesus knows what is coming, and He has gone up to the Mount of Olives to get ready spiritually. I can only imagine what He was thinking. He was about to be separated from His Father for the first time in eternity. He was about to be tested by the devil in ways He had never been tested before. He then speaks to His friends. He had loved all people, for sure—He had loved His disciples (the Twelve) absolutely—but now He is with His special friends, the Three. And Jesus pours His heart out to them.

> Then Jesus went with his disciples to a place called Gethsemane, and he said to them, "Sit here while I go over there and pray." He took Peter and the two sons of Zebedee along with him, and he began to be sorrowful and troubled. Then he said to them, "My soul is overwhelmed with sorrow to the point of death. Stay here and keep watch with me."
>
> Going a little farther, he fell with his face to the ground and prayed, "My Father, if it is possible, may this cup be taken from me. Yet not as I will, but as you will."
>
> Then he returned to his disciples and found them sleeping. "Couldn't you men keep watch with me for one hour?"

he asked Peter. "Watch and pray so that you will not fall into temptation. The spirit is willing, but the flesh is weak."

He went away a second time and prayed, "My Father, if it is not possible for this cup to be taken away unless I drink it, may your will be done."

Here is what is so astounding to me. I had always seen in Scripture the perfect way Jesus loved people. He courageously gave them what they needed to hear even when it cost Him. He showed compassion, humility, and self-sacrifice. But there is something more here. He wasn't just loving the disciples; He was being in relationship with them. He shared His struggle—yes, Jesus as man was struggling.

Sometimes we forget that God is relational and has feelings. We think of Him as perfect (and He is), but in our minds this means He cannot be hurt. Even Old Testament Scripture tells us that this is not true—Genesis says God's heart was grieved that He had even made man. We can grieve the Holy Spirit, we are told.

In Matthew 26, Jesus shares His pain with mere humans. He says, "Pray with me—sit with me." He then cries out to God with His struggle, and they are aware of it (they had to have been because they wrote about it for us). Jesus says, "Father, take this from me if it is possible. My God, is there another way? Please, Father, if it's possible change my path." Relationship means that we are honest and allow others into our struggle. To be in relationship means they get to love and support us too.

This wasn't the only time Jesus did this. He shared His frustration with God's people on numerous occasions. He wept over the death of Lazarus. As a man, Jesus needed to experience the life of faith as we do so He could understand us and become a merciful High Priest who intercedes for us.

As humans, we need others to help us on the journey of faith. Jesus was most certainly tasked with making disciples who could share the story with the world. (What good is the Greatest Story Ever Told if no one faithfully tells it?) But the disciples were also given to Jesus to help Him face Calvary and do the work He had been given to do. Relationship is the fuel that enables us to complete the task. Honest relationship means I love you, but it also means I share my life with you. And in so doing, I help you and you help me.

Pastors often tell me they need to have pastor prayer meetings with other local church leaders because in part it's the only place they can be real. Their thought is that no one else can understand their struggles. They feel that if people in their congregations knew they were struggling, their persona of perfection would be gone and they would lose their credibility.

While I think it's great to pray with other church leaders, I disagree with the premise that their people cannot understand. The King of the universe shared His struggles with mere uneducated fishermen (there couldn't be a greater distance between the two) and asked them to pray with Him. So what makes us think our people can't understand us and help us as we journey on our own God-given mission?

Scripture is clear that no sin has overtaken us that is not common to man (1 Cor. 10:13). We are all the same. We are broken. The devil loves to fill our heads with thoughts that will keep us isolated. When we are alone, he can distort our thinking. But when a pastor is real in sharing, he actually encourages others; they understand he is like them, and think, *If he can face it, so can I.* Paul shared his life with regular, everyday people. He shared that he had a thorn in the flesh. He reminded them that he had despaired until they encouraged him. He told them that in his sinful nature he was depraved and had a constant inner struggle going on.

Now, I understand the challenge. Loving difficult people is hard enough, but there is more to God's commands than just loving people. Real relationship means that we allow ourselves to be known, and, sure, this can really hurt. We don't want to become deeply involved in other people's lives. Other people have possibly sucked the life out of us and even hurt us when we shared intimate details that exposed us and the whole thing was handled badly. Why would we go down that road again? Why would we ever take a chance again? Why would we enter into inevitable pain and messiness?

Let me remind you that in the beginning (before the fall) relationships were easy. But because of sin the world is a mess. Yet our basic design demands relationship. It's a vicious circle. Because of sin, we find it hard to be in relationship with others. But we still feel this need deep within us. It's like we need to drink water to survive, but we don't want to drink water because we drank water once and then threw up. Now we're hesitant to ever drink water again. But we're so thirsty, so very thirsty. What do we do?

That's usually the big tension when it comes to loving people and being in relationship with them, isn't it? We know we're supposed to love people with the unconditional love of Christ, because that's what Jesus commanded. But be in relationship too? The people in our sphere of influence aren't always lovable. They annoy us. They frustrate us. The situation is messy. It's much easier to walk out the side door and call it quits than to work through relational difficulties.

Grace Delivered through Community

Remember that every command Jesus ever gave was for our good. He loves us and knows how He designed us. Just look at a few of the many Scriptures that show us what it means to have real relationships.

- "Therefore confess your sins to each other and pray for each other so that you may be healed. The prayer of a righteous person is powerful and effective" (James 5:16).
- "Do not lie to each other, since you have taken off your old self with its practices and have put on the new self, which is being renewed in knowledge in the image of its Creator" (Col. 3:9–10).
- "Carry each other's burdens, and in this way you will fulfill the law of Christ" (Gal. 6:2).

Confessing sins to one another. Being honest with one another. Carrying each other's burdens. These actions are all part of God's recipe for a spiritual life that can help you survive and thrive. So many have a faith like an eight-dollar Walmart tube because they cut themselves off from the plan God intended for us. We have a choice. Will we allow our past experiences to dictate our direction, or will we obey Jesus? When we allow past hurt and bitterness to dictate how we live, it's like that old analogy of a person driving a car while looking in his rearview mirror. Not only do you end up off the road in a ditch, but you manage to hurt others in your path. Jesus is asking us to do what is best for us, and this leaves us with a choice.

As I write this chapter, I'm in a particular home group with people, and none of them except me is a pastor. When we meet, I talk about my life with them, and they talk about their lives with me. (It's a mixed-gender group, so we do lay some ground rules about what is shared and not shared.) But there is more to it than that. I talk with the people in my home group three to five times per week, on average. I text them, and they text me. They come over to dinner at our house, and my wife and I have dinner at their houses. Sometimes the guys and I go hunting together. They regularly see me outside the context of teaching. I constantly share with them my hope for our relationships. I want to be real because I need them to pray for me and help me in my weaknesses. I guarantee they will see me at my worst because we are going to spend enough time together that they'll see me having a bad day. I guarantee them that I am going to need grace from them, and then invite them into being real with me also. As leaders and Christians, we constantly need to progress to where we're doing life together, asking each other how we're truly doing.

We have already looked at 1 Peter 4:10. Let's look at it in its full context, with verses 8 and 9:

> Above all, love each other deeply, because love covers over a multitude of sins. Offer hospitality to one another without grumbling. Each of you should use whatever gift you have received to serve others, as faithful stewards of God's grace in its various forms.

This passage reminds us that imperfect relationships are the norm, not the exception, and yet the Holy Spirit through

Scripture calls us to keep loving people anyway, to keep knowing people and being known. We are called to love one another deeply—from the heart (this is so much different than just being polite and surfacy), because love covers a multitude of sins. In fact, our depth of love for people is often revealed best when others let us down. If we love people only when they are easy to love, then our love has limited depth. Jesus called us to something better when He said that even pagans love those who love them. If we keep on loving people even when they're hard to love, our support can help give them the power to change. Not only that, but we develop greater strength and courage ourselves in the process. Just as God provides support for each other through physical families, He provides support through relationship in spiritual families.

The gifts we have been given from God are meant to be used within the spiritual family as vehicles of grace. We are to be managers and stewards of God's grace. Saving grace always comes from Christ and through Christ. Yet practical grace—the experience of grace for healing and restoration—often happens best through community.

When we sin, we are made pure because of what Jesus did on the cross. But sometimes it's hard to realize we've been forgiven. That's where real relationships come in. The Bible tells us to confess our sins to one another. Why? It's not so other people will wipe our slate clean with God—that's the work of Jesus—but so we might experience the practical outworking of grace. Other people can reassure us of God's love. Other people can help us cast our anxieties at the foot of the cross. We feel much "freer" after we've confessed sins to other people. God's grace often comes in the form of wisdom from other believers. God may answer our prayers for financial help through other believers. God's unmerited favor flows through people who help us even when we have made mistakes.

Many Christians do not really know the needs of others, and their own needs are not known either, because they have no deep spiritual relationships. Some will help others if they hear about the problems, but would feel embarrassed if anyone knew they also had marital issues or financial problems or whatever. This leaves us without God's delivery system for answering many prayers.

Over the years I have experienced what it looks like to not only accept Christ as Savior but as Lord. Once saved, I tried to face my addictions and depravity without the relationships that God's Word points us to. I failed to defeat my inner demons that had powerful strongholds in my life. But I have also experienced God's design and the victory that comes when I allowed the Holy Spirit, the Word of God, and the people of God to work in my daily battle. I have also seen the same victory in countless lives as well. Whether or not a Christian wins these real-life struggles is directly tied to their willingness to embrace authentic spiritual relationship.

In my own home I faced a struggle with a drug-addicted son that nearly destroyed not only his life but my marriage and ministry. The same kind of relationships that God used to lift me out of addiction are the kinds of relationships that carried me through the battles in my own heart and life. As I would be honest about my anger and frustration with my wife and son, and with a God who seemed to be distant, these friends would listen and support and encourage me. God used them to hold me together so that when my son came to his senses, he had something to come home to. God has truly given us all we need for life and godliness (2 Pet. 1:3)—and His plan is to use His people in relationship.

Staying the Course

A leader in my church led a home group awhile back that was absolutely crazy. He and his wife went around the neighborhood and asked everyone they met to come. Some who came were believers, but most had never followed Jesus.

Amazingly, within a few months, seven people decided to follow Christ and be baptized. We had a great celebration service in front of all their extended families, and the leader was excited. I immediately sat down with him and said, "I want you to imagine that you and your wife just had seven babies and have brought them home from the hospital. It's exciting, but now the hard work begins. I am warning you that life is about to get crazy for you and you are going to need help."

Sure enough, the next few seasons of life proved to be a messy time. There were conflicts within the group. There were misunderstandings. There was an overall immaturity—both spiritually and relationally.

But they kept at it. Two of the marriages were in big trouble, and the people in the group generally did not know how to love well—but they stayed the course. They didn't walk out the side door when the going got tough. They stayed intentional about growing their relationships and about being open and honest. Of course, the volunteer leader had to set the course because those in the group had no idea what it was supposed to look like. Since he and his wife were outnumbered (seven couples to one), they needed help at times. They freely admitted it and allowed others to help do the heavy lifting. That's real life. Two couples checked out even though they were pursued—it was heartbreaking and the leadership couple was tempted to give up. His wife was hurt because the women in the group could be mean. But the couple kept being faithful.

After a year, some of the messiness is finally beginning to be worked through. Several people in the group have experienced relationships for the first time as God has designed them. The leader is experiencing the strength that relationship can provide, and God is working in the lives of these families.

Maybe this chapter has been a big encouragement for you. You're in a tough relationship with a friend right now, but this chapter has given you a new vision for staying the course.

Or maybe you're not feeling encouraged. You're in a tough relationship with a friend, and you're reeling, wondering which way to turn, hoping things will one day get easier.

I find great encouragement in remembering that the power source for love and relationship is Christ. When we spend more time with Jesus, we see the perfect picture of love and we are encouraged. If we don't abide with Christ, then love becomes no more than a nice idea, because the Holy Spirit not only gives us directions for real love in the Word, but He is the gas that gives our relational car the energy to follow the directions on the road to relationship.

You can do this. Jesus calls you both to love people and to be in relationship with them. Take a risk. Cast a vision for relationship. Take the initiative to let yourself be known. And follow the model of Jesus.

5

Made for Family

In the same way a human being learns to be human in a family, a spiritual being learns to be spiritually mature in a spiritual family. God's Word tells us we are born again. Just as we get a spiritual Father when we become part of God's family, we get spiritual brothers and sisters, even spiritual sub-parents (under the Father) who help us grow up. So many people have been deprived of this, and just as human children without parents become impolite, socially awkward humans, so do spiritual children become spiritually and relationally awkward and destructive without a spiritual family to help them grow up.

Here's an example: A friend of mine shared a story with me that illustrates what I have been writing about. A couple in his church (I'll call them Brandon and Janice) had sponsored the middle school group at a friend's church for more than ten years and were good at attracting kids and keeping them busy. They truly loved the students in their care. Each Sunday morning and Wednesday evening they led the group, teaching Bible stories and opening and closing with crowd-breakers and games in the church's gym. Each spring and fall they took the kids to a denominational rally. Each summer they took the kids on a canoe trip. Each winter they took the kids on a snowshoe trip. The kids all liked Brandon and Janice a lot.

But there was a problem. While the middle school–aged kids all loved Brandon and Janice, the kids' parents consistently had a hard time with the couple. Not only did the kids' parents have a problem with them, so did the other leaders in the church. It seemed to this couple that they had the most important ministry and that the others should just move out of their way and let them serve. Brandon and Janice were basically both immature in their relationships with adults in general. Both had "sharp" personalities that could be grating, even abrasive. Communication lines got crossed often, which led to frustration and angst between leaders and parents. If confronted about a problem by parents, Brandon and Janice became defensive and dug in their heels. They were volunteers, after all, as they often reminded people when challenged on an issue. Who else was going to lead the middle school group if they didn't? They often suggested that the leaders of the church and the parents should appreciate their effort rather than criticize.

My friend, new on the church staff, began to examine the problem from the ground up. Brandon and Janice were in their early thirties and had five young children of their own, all under age eight. Brandon had a demanding, full-time job as a computer technician. Janice was a full-time homemaker who homeschooled the two oldest children. They were extremely busy people and often exhausted. That's where the problem began. Brandon worked all day long in a cubicle by himself. Janice took care of the kids all day in virtual isolation. In the evenings and on weekends, they saw and interacted with each other, but mainly planned events for the middle schoolers. That's all they ever had time to do. The extent of their spiritual connections was with middle school kids, so they needed to be the ones pouring into them and had no time to be poured into by mature Christians.

Bottom line: Brandon and Janice were so busy that they did not even know something was missing. Sometimes busyness can make you unaware that you are lonely. Down deep they longed for real relationships, although they didn't know how to articulate this longing. They had not really been discipled by anyone who lovingly challenged their behavior, so there were huge gaps in their lives. They didn't share (nor should they have shared) their deepest fears, struggles, temptations, and obstacles with the students they cared for, but they needed to be a part of the family of God whether or not they knew it. They were spiritual parents to the students, but they needed spiritual parents of their own to help grow them up into adult maturity. They needed spiritual brothers and sisters around their own age and stage of life to walk the road with them. Mature spiritual relationships are God's means for pouring into His people, and if you don't have that you are soon empty.

My friend was able to get Brandon and Janice out of their leadership position for a while and into a home group. (This wasn't easy, because often the very thing that is killing people is what they hold on to with a death grip.) Brandon and Janice found the changeover awkward and almost left the church over it. But fortunately they submitted to spiritual authority and, with help, trusted that the change was for their good. They courageously stuck it out. Soon they discovered what they had been missing. Within their home group, they began to grow up themselves. They were loved in spite of immaturity and social quirkiness, and because of that love in their lives, they learned how to be more mature. They began to share their lives with others and become better listeners and communicators. They experienced God's grace offered to them through other people, and they were able to administer God's grace to others. Through the group's loving confrontation, most of their rough edges gradually got sanded away. Because this couple was loved by others, they learned the importance of real biblical relationship.

Three years later, they returned to leadership of the middle school group, but this time things were changed. They shared the leadership responsibility with another couple, easing their own busyness. They also now recognized the need to abide in Christ personally in quiet times and through relationships with other spiritually mature believers. They slowed down their time spent on youth group activities so that they could stay committed to their home group. Just as an axe works better when it is sharp, these changes made the work they did with the youth more effective. They'd learned how to love in a family where real relationships could be lived out. They weren't "grown up" completely yet, but they were on the path toward true spiritual maturity.

Together in the Family of God

Yes, a church does have an organized time of worship in a specific location for a reoccurring period of time. But do you realize church is supposed to be much more than that? God's church is supposed to be a group of people in relationship who do life together. Relationships aren't simply a means to an end. Relationships are intrinsically important because the gospel gets lived out within those relationships. We were created to be loved and to love others. The relationships matter because in relationships we learn to be relational, and those relationships give us the power to live out the information we have learned.

Remember that a spiritually mature person loves God and loves others well. A mature person is known by others and knows others well. This is why God calls His church the family of God. The early church met together in the temple courts (large group settings), but also met together in homes where they were devoted to *koinōnea*—deep abiding relationship. They became spiritual family. Consider the qualities of a healthy family expressed in Acts 2:42 and following. They ate together, shared their possessions, and even sold their possessions if needed to care for each other. They focused on the Word of God and the apostles' teachings. A home group isn't simply a device that Christians can use to enhance knowledge about the Bible. A home group is a place where people can be relationally discipled as part of a spiritual family.

Consider the "family" language found throughout Scripture.

- **We are children of God.** "See what great love the Father has lavished on us, that we should be called children of

God! And that is what we are! The reason the world does not know us is that it did not know him. Dear friends, now we are children of God, and what we will be has not yet been made known. But we know that when Christ appears, we shall be like him, for we shall see him as he is" (1 John 3:1–2).

- **We are a family of believers.** "Therefore, as we have opportunity, let us do good to all people, especially to those who belong to the family of believers" (Gal. 6:10).

- **We are members of God's household, a corporate dwelling place for the Holy Spirit.** "Consequently, you are no longer foreigners and strangers, but fellow citizens with God's people and also members of his household, built on the foundation of the apostles and prophets, with Christ Jesus himself as the chief cornerstone. In him the whole building is joined together and rises to become a holy temple in the Lord. And in him you too are being built together to become a dwelling in which God lives by his Spirit" (Eph. 2:19–22).

- **We're all in this together.** "If one part suffers, every part suffers with it; if one part is honored, every part rejoices with it" (1 Cor. 12:26).

- **We are part of a living, spiritual household.** "If I am delayed, you will know how people ought to conduct themselves in God's household, which is the church of the living God, the pillar and foundation of the truth" (1 Tim. 3:15). The language of the writers of the New Testament reveals that they felt we are part of a spiritual family. Romans 1:13 says, "I do not want you to be unaware, brothers and sisters."

And this is only a sampling of verses. Family imagery is found throughout Scripture, particularly in the New Testament. A family lives together, prays together, grows together, and supports each other. I love Ephesians 4:14–16, where Paul describes how everyone in the family of God is important. In 1 Corinthians 12:12–26, Paul says everyone has work to do. And God explicitly calls Himself our Father and describes us as His sons and daughters in 2 Corinthians 6:18.

I mentioned earlier that the devil can grab hold of a word and distort its meaning. The word *family* has certainly been distorted by the devil. No one has grown up with a perfect family, that's for sure. We all are broken in ways that affect the family negatively. Some fathers abuse or abandon their wives and children. Some wives leave their homes or are emotionally abusive. Some siblings are cruel to one another. Some children are disobedient to parents. That's sin at work. But God is in the business of redemption. Whatever your experience with family has been, I encourage you to press on toward the ideal family of God described in the Bible. Let your experiences and definitions be rooted in the Bible, and allow God to start a new thing in your generation, both in and through you. Let Jesus redefine for you what "family" truly means. The family you came from is not as important as the family God helps you create.

Begin to look into Scripture to glean truth about our amazing heavenly Father and His family. For instance, 1 John 3:1–2 says that the family of God is rooted and established in great love. Not in hate. Not in desperation. Not in angst or stress or anxiety or fear or abuse. But in love. Let's read this passage again:

See what great love the Father has lavished on us, that we should be called children of God! And that is what we are! The reason the world does not know us is that it did not know him. Dear friends, now we are children of God, and what we will be has not yet been made known. But we know that when Christ appears, we shall be like him, for we shall see him as he is.

Maybe you wonder why you have not experienced this— not in your childhood home nor in the church. That is the point of this book: most of us have not. That's why the church has struggled to make a difference in a world where people need what God designed them for. Within the church itself, many have lost hope that it can be different. Christians tend to either settle for the status quo or leave the church for a form of spirituality that was not God's idea. Either way, many believers are not experiencing what God had in mind, and this breaks God's heart.

The point is this: Although the enemy deceives us by stealing our words and changing definitions, it is our job to become a spiritual family who restores truth, including the definition of the word *family* God gives us. It's our job in our home groups to live out a family relationship that new disciples can see and then live it out further as families are restarted with God's way of living. Natural physical families can be restored as disciple-making machines when we begin in the spiritual family, in the church, done God's way.

In 1 Timothy 5, the Holy Spirit through Paul lays out for us the privileges and responsibilities of the family of God. Paul, now an older pastor, writes to Timothy, a younger pastor, encouraging him to teach the people in his congregation about true relationships. Here are a few of the directives Paul gives to Timothy about how a loving family should function.

- Do not rebuke an older man harshly, but exhort him as if he were your father.
- Treat younger men as brothers.
- Treat older women as mothers.
- Treat younger women as sisters, with absolute purity.
- Take care of widows, and encourage the families of widows to look after the widows themselves.

This is family language, and love is the goal. Think about relationships between parents and children. Fathers guide, encourage, and direct. Mothers nurture, train, and support. That's what older believers can do for us. Think about the relationships between brothers and sisters. Brothers and sisters are there to be on each other's side. They encourage each other, defend and protect each other, joke around with each other. Godly brothers and sisters can tell us what we need to hear rather than what we want to hear when we are getting off track. Not because they want to be right but because they love us.

Living Examples

As a spiritual family, we have Jesus as our model. We have God's Word to unpack the truths of Jesus's identity and mission, and to give us direction. Godly brothers and sisters provide living examples to watch and to follow. People who have grown up spiritually, who are ahead of us in the faith, model what it looks like to know and to be known.

Paul offers this example to us in several Scriptures. You would expect Paul to point everything toward Jesus, and he does, ultimately. Yet at least twice Paul points to himself and calls himself a model for others to follow, as he follows Christ.

In Philippians 4:9 Paul says, "Whatever you have learned or received or heard from me, or seen in me—put it into practice. And the God of peace will be with you." Paul is pointing directly to himself here. He's saying, "Look at my life. Look at the things I do. Learn from me. Do things the way I do them, because my life is an example of what it looks like to be a Christian."

In Philippians 3:17 Paul says, "Join together in following my example, brothers and sisters, and just as you have us as a model, keep your eyes on those who live as we do." That's a spiritual family in practice.

Hebrews 13:7 says, "Remember your leaders, who spoke the word of God to you. Consider the outcome of their way of life and imitate their faith." That's good spiritual mentorship at work. We are to look to Christ ultimately, and also look to spiritual leaders—not for salvation, but as examples of how to faithfully live out the Christian faith. This is why spending time together is so important—if we don't get to see how people really live out their faith in practice, we are losing the best form of teaching: modeling.

I was a prodigal son who ran from my spiritual Father as well as my earthly parents for a long time. I embarrassed my dad especially, as he was a pastor in a church. I soiled his reputation but couldn't care less. Yet my father never stopped loving me. In tangible ways he and my mom walked the tension between enabling me and standing for truth. They never approved of my sin nor supported it in any way, and yet they pursued me and never let me forget that the road back home was open. When my road finally led to emptiness and destruction, my parents were still there to welcome me home and help me walk with Jesus.

When my son followed my pattern and hurt himself, and Lori and me as parents, I had an example to look to, so I knew what to do. My father had not only been a model for me but supported me as I was going through it. He shared with me what he had thought when I was dragging him through the mud and reminded me that God was faithful and that I could have hope. He helped me stay resolute yet grace-filled for my son, both through his encouragement and the model he had been earlier in my life. My father reached out to my son when I could not. He was my spiritual father when I was young and became my spiritual colaborer on my parenting journey.

My dad and mom were not the only examples to Lori and me. Over the years God has given us many spiritual family members who have invested in us. Several years ago my wife and I were feeling crushed under the weight of financial decisions made in college. By the time I had come to Christ I had destroyed my credit and had huge bills that were hard to manage. Neither I nor my wife had been trained in how to handle money well. (My father was a pastor and never had much to manage.) We took side jobs to make ends meet, which strained our marriage because we were already working hard in ministry and with our own young children.

One day an older man in the church asked me why I had been so stressed lately. I shared that we were struggling financially. He asked if he and his wife could come and talk to Lori and me. That night they spent hours going through our budget, identifying overspending, and talking about how we could manage our finances differently. They acted like spiritual parents to us. They didn't give us any prideful lectures. There were no challenges to our dignity. They simply offered wise words that encouraged us to believe there was a way out of the mess. They offered to let us live in their rental to reduce our overhead. They offered to meet with us once a month to talk about how we were doing financially.

That's how the body of Christ can act. This older, wiser couple was willing to do far more than merely give good advice. They became spiritual family members who gave their time and resources to help.

What Families Do

Have you noticed how people tend to have big expectations for what happens at church? We want churches to be perfect. We want the services to be well done and inspirational. We want the worship experience to move us. We want programs and ministries that connect us and our kids to the Lord better. We want to be recognized and known by staff members and leaders (or at least for our names to be known). We want to get along with everybody, and we want people to consistently treat us well. Overall, we want churches to be effective, professionally run, and filled with people who don't disappoint us. But people inevitably do disappoint us, and we're tempted to become disillusioned when things aren't perfect. Either that or we leave and try to find perfection at another church. If enough churches disappoint us, then we create a form of faith that's about just me and Jesus, on the golf course or in the woods—no people.

It's a game changer when we realize that churches are meant to be much less about being businesses that provide quality customer service and much more about being families that we're a part of, for better or worse. We don't "go" to church. We "are" the church. And families aren't perfect. Far from it. Families—even Christian families—are real. They are filled with imperfect people who are redeemed by God's love and grace and forgiveness. I often remind people that the letters inspired by the Holy Spirit in the New Testament were written to churches that had gotten off track. Every writer challenged and encouraged those in the church to be all that God called them to be as members of His family.

Here are three characteristics of real, God-honoring spiritual families. Remind yourself of these the next time something doesn't go perfectly at church.

1. Families love each other no matter what.

When you were a kid and you spilled your milk at the dinner table, did your parents stop loving you? Of course not. They might have become annoyed or reprimanded you, particularly if it was the thirtieth time in a week that you'd spilled your milk, but the love didn't stop. Not in a good family, anyway. Certainly some of us experienced abusive families where we were uncertain about the love our parents had for us. But in families centered on Christ, love never goes away. Similarly, the love of God never changes for us. If we are Jesus's disciples, God is our heavenly Father, and He always loves us no matter what we do. In Malachi 3:6 God boldly says, "I the LORD do not change." And in Jeremiah 31:3 God says He loves us with "an everlasting love." God calls us to have this same type of love for our brothers and sisters in Christ.

As I wrote earlier, love is an act of the will, and our depth of love is revealed not just when relationships are smooth and people are reciprocating love, but when people have failed us. That's when we are called to love anyway. And that's what's supposed to happen in godly families. It's easy to love people when they are kind and gracious to us; even the pagans do that. But it's much more difficult to love people when they aren't being kind or considerate or gracious. Yet that's what we are called to do within our churches: love people anyway.

If you are waiting to let yourself be known only when others prove themselves to be perfect people who never disappoint you, then you will wait a long time. You will never be known. As mentioned earlier, we are hardwired for deep connection. We need to be known, and to lack that leaves us vulnerable to physical and spiritual problems. To love, and to be in relationships where you risk being honest with others—that's what we are called to do in a family. But people disappoint and hurt us when we allow them to be close and are authentic. This is why forgiveness is a necessity for believers. Relationship takes commitment that overshadows difficulty.

Let's cast the vision within our churches: We must put down our façades and live honestly. The vision needs to reach everyone in the family, but especially spiritual leaders who set the tone. Then we must beat the drum over and over that families love each other no matter what, that we forgive when we are hurt, share feelings honestly when this happens, and resolve conflicts lovingly rather than go underground with our pain. We are warned to not let the sun go down on our anger, which gives the devil a foothold. The devil is the enemy of relationship and will use any opportunity to divide the family through bitterness. Hebrews tells us to not let a bitter root grow that will defile many, because it will ruin relationships, destroying our ability to live strongly and be the testimony to Jesus's power we are called to be. We might disagree with someone, or someone might be disappointed with us, but we're still in the family of God together. God is still our Father. We are still sisters and brothers. Real love requires willingness to overlook imperfections, forgive, and give each other the benefit of the doubt. "[Love] always protects, always trusts, always hopes, always perseveres" (1 Cor. 13:7).

2. Families help prevent problems from happening.

When people walk into my office and tell me something's wrong in their lives (maybe their marriage is on the rocks), one of the first things I ask is how the problem got to this point. Usually they just want the problem to be fixed immediately. And in their minds the best way for that to happen is if the other person does the changing. But there's a greater issue at stake—and if they can understand and wrestle with this greater issue, it can help ward off future problems.

See, real relationships have a "preventative" quality. We need to be in real relationship with others to prevent our problems from getting to the point of crisis. Real relationship means we consistently share problems with each other when those problems are still small. People are praying for us. We're praying for others. There's a lot of mutual support and encouragement. Day-to-day interaction with others helps us along the way.

Being part of a quality small group is like doing preventative maintenance on your car. You can buy a car straight off the lot and drive it until it drops. But that same car will last a whole lot longer if you regularly take it to the mechanic's shop. Technicians will change the oil, rotate the tires, change the coolant in the radiator, and perform a host of other services. You don't simply take your car to the mechanic once. You take it in regularly, every three thousand to five thousand miles. Preventative care is ongoing; you always need preventative maintenance done on your car. The same is true for our spiritual lives.

When a home group is constantly around you, and when the people are constantly encouraging you along your spiritual journey, it's much harder for little problems to become big problems because of a lack of awareness. Not only do you share the problems you think you have, but they notice the ones you don't see because they are around enough to see who you really are. They then in love help correct your course before it takes you off the right road to a dead end. But you have to desire this kind of accountability for others to be willing to give it. If you are defensive when others confront your brokenness, they will either leave you the way you are or just leave you. Though it's true that we need others to look past our faults and love us anyway, love tells us the truth, too, when our brokenness is hurting us and others.

Years ago in one home group I was in, we were all sharing our stuff, and a man talked about how he struggled with porn. (We'd separated the men and women that night, so we could talk about deeper struggles.) When the man shared this, several of us immediately said, "Okay, how can we help you?" There was no condemnation from us. That's not what a family is about. There was only encouragement and prayer.

The man, who was new to the home group, said, "What do you mean . . . help?"

One of our guys said, "Well, let's put a filter on your computer. Let's set up an accountability system. Let's create a plan to help you in this area of struggle. That type of thing."

The man sort of balked and said, "Nah, I think I can handle just not looking at it again." Besides, he said, he needed his computer, and some filters might keep him from being able to go where he needed to go to do his job. "I just wanted to be honest with you guys about my struggles," he said.

I could tell he was offended and had deliberately guided the conversation away from the topic. Later on I continued the conversation in private, and as I'd suspected, he was mad enough about it that he didn't want to come back to the group. He shared that he felt judged because the guys had immediately pushed him toward action. I shared with him that the one doing the most talking about the subject had dealt with this same issue in our group in the last home group season. He was leaning hard because he knew how porn could destroy his relationship with God and his wife. He almost lost all he cared about, and he didn't want this outcome for the man who had opened up. He had just recently experienced the freedom he had wanted for years. He had shared with us, and then we had challenged and encouraged him to do all that he was now suggesting, and it had worked. The man wasn't judging; he was excited.

After explaining all this to the offended man, I asked him a question. "Do you think real relationship means just listening to problems and not doing anything to help?" I asked him if he understood real accountability. I shared with him that in our group we care enough to help each other back on the path toward wholeness.

I explained that it's not enough to just be honest about your brokenness. You also have to be willing to lean into the direction God wants you to go. The Holy Spirit will give you power to change ultimately, yet you need to paddle your surfboard in the direction of the wave. I explained how the Holy Spirit uses His people to point you in the right direction to paddle.

Sometimes we don't want people to hold us accountable or speak truth into our lives. We just want people to listen to us. And sure, sometimes people will simply do that, and it's a start. But we need to be willing to take action too. The Bible lays out strong words for us in Hebrews 3:12–13:

> See to it, brothers and sisters, that none of you has a sinful, unbelieving heart that turns away from the living God. But encourage one another daily, as long as it is called "Today," so that none of you may be hardened by sin's deceitfulness.

Note the good "family" language in that passage. "See to it, *brothers and sisters*," the writer of Hebrew says. He understands that families help prevent problems. And one way families do this is to "encourage one another daily." The word for "encourage" here in the Greek is *parakaleō*, the same word that describes the function of the Holy Spirit. The word means more than merely being a cheerleader for somebody. It connotes a true and strong helper, Someone who comforts, consoles, exhorts, admonishes, and persuades.

Families help each other out by "encouraging" one another in the larger sense of the word.

That function of true encouragement helps prevent a whole host of problems later on.

3. Families are restorative.

When a family member goes astray, the family doesn't just say "See ya!" and turn their back on the one who has gone off course. There may come a time to separate, but that's the last resort and even then separation is done in hopes that the person will come to their senses and return to the Lord and the spiritual family. When that person is in your family, you just wait and look for a glimpse of hope that the rest of your family can help restore that member to Jesus, life, health, and wholeness.

When things don't go as planned, we must have the courage to fight for our relationships. The devil constantly strives to separate us from each other because there is strength in numbers. We must fight to understand each other, forgive, extend grace, and restore each other to Jesus. Just as I shared with the older couple who had been married for fifty years, we are called to love that way in the church—we are the family of God.

Far Off on the Horizon

Remember, within the family of God, our love toward others must be based on a decision rather than a feeling. Just as a parent cares for a child who is sick in the night whether or not that parent feels like it, a spiritual family member cares for those in the family. Not just the pastors, but everyone must learn to be part of a spiritual culture we share together.

When one of the women in my home group lost her husband recently, it was amazing to watch how other women surrounded her as friends. It was apparent that they spoke together several times a week and did much more than just go to church together. One woman watched the new widow's two small children so she could go to school and train to find a way to care for the family's needs.

Another woman's husband left her and her kids last year, and to hear her speak about her spiritual family was awesome. The men in our group cut wood for her, and some of the women texted her every morning to check on her. She said that she has never felt so supported and loved. It was so gratifying for me to know that it was not me doing most of the pastoring in this group. Every person understood their role as a spiritual brother or sister, and this culture carried these people in crises through them.

The woman whose husband left her invited another couple to our home group, and they told me they had come to try to understand the strength this woman had, where it came from. Imagine—she is in the hardest spot you can be in, yet she is being a light to others because she has strength they could not understand. They had heard about her best friend, Jesus, and also about her spiritual family in her church. They realized something was missing in their lives.

At the same meeting, two of our men were making plans for hunting season, and the rest of the guys talked about the men's group we attend together on Wednesday morning. For a pastor, moments like this make it worthwhile—when people are growing up spiritually and becoming what they were saved to be.

That's what doing life together as a family can be like. We see each other when we're down. We don't hide from each other. We do life together and help each other along the way.

Christians are not perfect, no. We are saved by the Lord, given new hearts and minds, and encouraged to walk in the pathway of Jesus. To be mature and Christlike means that we walk the road with imperfect people.

That's what it means to be in the family of God.

6

Pride: The Spiritual Family Killer

Whenever I discuss the need for real relationships, some people think I'm advocating that we create church environments where we simply listen to each other and don't respond or correct. We become good listeners, and that's it—a kind of group counseling session where we don't dive into the Scriptures or challenge wrong thinking or actions. But as I briefly explained in the last chapter, that's not what I mean. Yes, we need to listen well, but we also need intentionally built relationships that can withstand hard truth when it needs to be spoken. I don't advocate a one-way street where the leader gets to be the expert. A good group is led by a mature leader who guides and facilitates and who is filled with the humility of knowing they can learn from others. As Scripture tells us in Ephesians 5:21, we need to submit to each other out of reverence for Christ.

Submission is almost a dirty word to many in our American culture today, but I want to stress that the concept is not a reason to get our hackles up. In America, the idea of democracy is drilled into us from a young age, and democracy is a good thing when we're dealing with governments and overthrowing dictatorships and that sort of thing. But it's not so good when we're dealing with our spiritual lives.

See, the concept of democracy is based around the idea that we have a right to speak into everything and the majority rules. If I think the majority is wrong, then I can break away and rule myself or start something new. There is tension here. As believers, we are called to follow Jesus above every other authority, and if the world commands us to disobey God, then we must choose Jesus. But too often even for Christians pride and rebellion have become the norm—even in issues of secondary importance. I live in North Idaho, where you might see a pickup truck going down the highway with a bumper sticker that says "My Master Is a Jewish Carpenter," then right beside it on the same bumper is another sticker that says "You Can Take My Gun When You Pry It from My Cold, Dead Fingers." That's the "I am in charge" mind-set at work.

That rebel culture might have worked well when John Adams led the charge to dump tea into Boston Harbor in defiance of the British Tea Act of 1773. But in many places in modern society (particularly in our spiritual lives) that attitude will get us into a lot of spiritual trouble. Our American culture has created a defiance toward police officers, parents, teachers, and government officials. We see the wrong kind of rebellion throughout our modern culture. Unfortunately, it has affected Christians as well, so defiance can even be found in church. People say (or at least think) things like,

If I don't like what you have to say, church leaders, then I don't need to listen to you. I submit to Jesus, not to a pastor or a church leader.

But what does the Bible have to say about this?

My Way or the Highway

Ephesians 5:21 lays out a different mind-set and way of living for us. We are to "submit to one another out of reverence for Christ." There's that word we don't like again—*submit*. The Greek word for "submit" is *hypotassō*. It means to let others positively influence or lead us. We deliberately submit ourselves to the godly counsel of others. Paul told Timothy (the appointed leader of a church Paul started) to teach, rebuke, encourage, and guide. He even told Timothy to command certain men to stop behaving the way they were. Paul's words placed an authority on Timothy. So my question is this: If Paul told Timothy to lead and gave him direction about how to do it, then what would he say to those in Timothy's congregation? It seems pretty obvious—they were to submit to Timothy's leadership.

Second Timothy 3:1–5 issues a strong warning for us:

> But mark this: There will be terrible times in the last days. People will be lovers of themselves, lovers of money, boastful, proud, abusive, disobedient to their parents, ungrateful, unholy, without love, unforgiving, slanderous, without self-control, brutal, not lovers of the good, treacherous, rash, conceited, lovers of pleasure rather than lovers of God—having a form of godliness but denying its power. Have nothing to do with such people.

We see the sort of defiance and rebellion described here in churches today. The mind-set and practice often reflect the opposite of true and godly submission. Christians love themselves more than they love God. Christians love money and are greedy to get more. Christians boast about their accomplishments and gifting. Christians can be abusive. Christians can be ungrateful. Christians can be proud and refuse to obey the leaders in their spiritual families and countries' governments. And the list goes on and on.

Lack of submission is further pressed in Protestant churches (though I see few Catholics submitting as well). I lead a Protestant church, and I love our church body dearly. Yet Protestants aren't known for submitting to any sort of church hierarchy either. Our mind-set and practices are rooted in "protesting," and we tend to take the verses about the priesthood of all believers a bit too far. We're suspicious of any sort of hierarchy or leadership that commands us to do anything, and we tend to insinuate that a leader is building a cult if he tries to exert the God-given authority given to him. Church people vote with their feet. The attitude is, *If I don't like things at this church, then I'll leave and go to the church down the street.* Of course, we use spiritual language to cover up our rebellion. We say things like, "I am part of the church universal, so I don't need to submit to any local church leadership."

Let me just say this boldly and firmly: That attitude is *wrong.* It's spiritually rebellious. First Samuel 15:23 says strongly, "For rebellion is like the sin of divination, and arrogance like the evil of idolatry." Do you know what divination is? It's witchcraft. That's how strongly the Bible condemns rebellion. Whenever we rebel against godly authority, it's as if we had sworn allegiance to Satan. Rebellion is the language of the devil, not of Jesus, who submitted to His Father and even to earthly leaders He had helped create. And arrogance is just as bad as worshiping idols. That's how strongly that verse pushes us toward a different mind-set of godly living. What's the opposite of arrogance? It's godly humility. What's the opposite of rebellion? It's godly submission.

Sometimes Christians feel that they can't submit to church leadership because there have been past abuses in that area. Maybe you went to a church that insisted you follow man-made rules, and if you didn't follow the rules, the church condemned you. Spiritual abuse is real, and it does happen today, so we always need to be discerning. Yet I encourage you to take a fresh look at Ephesians 5:21, at this instruction to "submit [ourselves] to one another," and look at it in the context of loving, supportive, godly relationships.

Loving God and others means that we are real, open, and honest with one another. We aren't prideful. We don't judge others. We don't condemn or coerce or manipulate others. We walk the road together. Hebrews 3:13 exhorts us to "encourage one another daily . . . so that none of [us] may be hardened by sin's deceitfulness." Remember, *encourage* also means to exhort or admonish—meaning that we seek and listen to wise counsel when it is supported in Scripture. That's an example of submitting to one another. As we saw earlier, when we truly "encourage" each other, we do more than cheer each other on. We hold forth wisdom. We spur one another on to righteousness.

Believers are also encouraged to obey leaders. Hebrews 13:7 tells us to "remember your leaders, who spoke the word of God to you. Consider the outcome of their way of life and imitate their faith." This encourages us to be loyal to our leaders; attentively observe the way they live; take notes on their convictions, conduct, and heart attitudes; and then imitate them. The writer of Hebrews then commands obedience: "Have confidence in your leaders and submit to their authority, because they keep watch over you as those who must give an account. Do this so that their work will be a joy, not a burden, for that would be of no benefit to you" (Heb. 13:17).

God has established leaders who are given the responsibility to protect and lead, and those in the body are called to follow and support. The key here is humility, definitely one of the characteristics of a mature believer. This is how Christ encourages us to live. Philippians 2:1–5 says,

> Therefore if you have any encouragement from being united with Christ, if any comfort from his love, if any common sharing in the Spirit, if any tenderness and compassion, then make my joy complete by being like-minded, having the same love, being one in spirit and of one mind. Do nothing out of selfish ambition or vain conceit. Rather, in humility value others above yourselves, not looking to your own interests but each of you to the interests of the others.
>
> In your relationships with one another, have the same mindset as Christ Jesus.

Note that if a person disagrees on a core theological issue, then it's okay to part ways. However, we must be careful to rightly divide the difference between a core salvation issue and an issue that is disputable. We can agree to disagree about some things and still be part of the same family working together for God's glory. However, even when it may be time to leave, we never have the right to fight like the devil for the things of God. We are called to be kind even to our enemy, so how much more must we be kind to someone who is a fellow believer. Too many churches divide over issues that aren't core. The issues are stylistic or matters of preference. We must continually fight against that kind of division in our churches. We need to be comfortable with going to a church where we might not totally see eye to eye with everybody on every single issue. We may disagree on how to minister in a community (should we do singles' or seniors' ministry?). We may disagree about the color of the carpet or how frequently we use hymns or choruses.

So be it. We disagree. It's perfectly okay to be part of a church where we wish some things were different. We are still called on to trust our leaders and obey them. We are still called to be kind and gentle with the people with whom we disagree. They're our brothers and sisters in the Lord. We are still gracious with them, and hopefully they with us. In the words of Ephesians 4:3, "Make every effort to keep the unity of the Spirit through the bond of peace." Remember that true love perseveres—it never quits—and we are only mature if we love that way.

At Real Life, our number one objective is to get people into deep relational environments where discipleship happens. We believe this happens best when we can see how a person functions in the most important parts of their lives, including the home life. When we looked at our women's ministry, we found that most of our women were involved only in the numerous events, classes, and relational groups, which didn't include husbands or children. Now, we were not against women getting together, but activity can take the place of deep spiritual relationship and growth. Rather than both, we were getting just one and not the most important one. Bottom line, many of our women were too busy in those activities to be in a home group, so their husbands were not part of one either. Every spiritually mature woman knows if the family is truly to be spiritually well led, then she, as a wife, cannot be the only one who is growing spiritually. The husband must grow into a spiritually mature man as well.

Even when a woman was involved in both women's ministry *and* a home group, it led to harried, shallow forms of relationship for her, because it takes time to really know and be known.

Part of our problem was that as a church we offered too many good things. It was separating families. So we reorganized our entire women's ministry as part of our overall strategy. Do you know how difficult it is to reorganize an entire ministry with hundreds of volunteers and thousands of participants? But we made some difficult decisions, prioritizing the way we did things. We decided to change our women's ministry priority to having mixed-gender home groups that met weekly. We would blend what had been three silos (home groups, men's ministries, and women's ministries) into one ministry that worked together to create disciples in the church who could then help the home to become the disciple-making entity it was supposed to be. The goal would be to have the home groups meet weekly, but one or two nights a month (during home-group time) they would break into men's and women's groups separately within the home. The women would go deeper into women's issues. We knew most of these women would meet some other time a couple of times a month as well, and our hope would be that they would attend the few events we still did in women's ministry together.

This would mean that rather than being in several groups with different women, they would most often be with the same women so they could go deeper into relationship. They would get to really know each other so that the more mature women would help the younger, less mature to grow spiritually. The men would do the same, enabling us to get men and women to the same group where real relationships could be formed as couples and families. This would allow the leader to see how the man or woman dealt with their spouse and children. Real discipleship could happen in every sphere of a person's life as a result.

To pull this off we had to explain the issues to the Women's Ministry department leaders, and believe me, this was a process, because they had built an amazing ministry dedicated to women.

Of course, some didn't like the change. I expected that. Nobody likes change, even at the best of times. Some people felt shut down. Some people felt overlooked. Some leaders came to us, saying, "We don't quite understand this. Would you explain it to us?" So we explained it again, hopefully communicating more clearly what we were trying to do and why. In the end, most of the leaders said, "Okay, we get what we're trying to do as a church. And we're for it." They asked if they could share a different way than we had initially come up with, and we knew they understood the women's issues better than we did. So we said yes. In time we worked together to come up with an even better way than we started with. Others said, "We don't like it, but we understand the change and we'll submit to the overall authority and direction the church leaders desire." And they did. They didn't get mad and storm off to another church. Of course, some were immature and decided to find a place that would let them do what they wanted to do, but not nearly as many as we had thought would. The depth of spiritual maturity was amazing to me and to our team.

That's exactly what we need to do as churches and individuals. If we don't like something, we need to talk it out, always forbearing with one another. We patiently work out solutions, continually gracious with one another. It's far too easy to get mad and shout, or walk out and slam the door. It's easy to take our ball and go home and not say a word, thinking that is maturity. That kind of person says, "I was mature because I didn't cause a fight, I just left." But how is there submission to leadership in such a stance? But such expressions of anger only burn bridges; they don't build understanding, and they certainly do not bring glory to God or attract a broken world in need of real relationships.

Sometimes after sharing and discussing we just don't see eye to eye. Sometimes we must choose to accept that ultimately those God has put in charge are responsible to Him and we need to obey them. Obviously this only goes so far—if someone is asking us to do something morally or ethically wrong, we can't, but so often people divide over what curriculum we use, what book we read, or the style of preaching—non-core issues. Spiritual maturity levels are revealed in the way we respond when our authority asks us to do something we do not understand or like.

Many scriptural passages support this. In Proverbs 9:7–9, we are told that wise people add to their wisdom when rebukes and additional teaching are accepted and heeded. Romans 13:1–7 urges us to submit to governing authorities, "for there is no authority except that which God has established"

(v. 1). Again, in Ephesians 5:21 we are told to "submit to one another out of reverence for Christ." We actually glorify God when we submit to one another. In Hebrews 13:17 we are told to submit to our leaders' authority. When we do so, their work becomes "a joy, not a burden," and that actually benefits us in the end.

Leading out of Reverence for Christ

Timothy's task was to lead the church and use the gift he was given by the authority of the elders. But Paul also tells him to embrace the right attitude as he leads. He tells Timothy to lead older men as he would his father and older women as mothers, and so on. Paul tells him to love them like family but that his task is also to lead just as the church's task is to follow. Between the lines Paul is telling Timothy to lead for the good of the family and not his personal ego or gain. There can be no ego-driven dictators in the church.

Leaders must be submissive too. This might sound counterintuitive at first, but it's not in practice. If leaders are submissive, to whom do they submit? The answer is that leaders must be submissive to God, other leaders, and even other Christians. Yes, it takes strong leadership to get a church off the ground, and yes, it takes strong leadership to keep a church running smoothly. But Ephesians 5:21, which says "Submit to one another out of reverence for Christ," applies to everyone, not just people who aren't in leadership positions.

A major goal in our church is to reach younger families. But as I have grown older, the demographic I naturally and effectively reach has grown older along with me. So our leadership team has purposely brought in our younger pastors to preach. Yes, we had a good reason for doing this, but no, not everybody liked it. When we first started having younger pastors preach, some people in the congregation said to me, "Jim, we like your preaching best. We don't want to listen to these younger guys. We don't get anything out of their sermons." So I explained the vision to reach younger families and grow up potential leaders. We did not want to become a personality-driven church. Most people accepted and understood our elders' decision. Others told me that although they understood, they didn't like it and chose to leave, again revealing their spiritual maturity level.

As I read through Scripture, it seems to me that Christians ought not to act that way. That's rebellion. See, I decided to bring in younger pastors in consultation with our eldership team. I didn't simply dictate the decision. Paul told Titus (Titus 1:5) to appoint elders in every town—plural. One person should not rule the church even if they are spiritually mature, because no one person has eyes to see every nuance of strategy. No one person has all the abilities a church body is supposed to have. The church leadership as a whole in our church had prayed about it for some time, then decided to go the direction of inviting the young to play a larger role. So the people who left weren't submitting to our church leadership. More than that, I don't think they were submitting to God, who speaks to and through a leadership team through prayer and the Word. Those who left were thinking with a "me and I" mentality and "a spiritual democracy" mind-set and voting with their feet. And that's not what Christ tells us to do.

Sure, I've seen fathers, bosses, and pastors who are dictators—it's *their way or the highway*—and that is unbiblical and never works well. Pastors in particular who think like this tend to either become deeply entrenched in their churches and ultimately drive people away, or become frustrated and bounce from church to church when leadership recognizes their immaturity. Pastors need to commit to listening and submitting to their eldership. They also must understand that the people in the church can be used by God to speak to the leadership as well. A good parent doesn't let the young kids in the backseat of the car dictate the family's travel plans, or meal schedule, or menu for the week. However, a good parent can learn much from the kids as well. Some of my greatest lessons have come from my kids. They have said things to me that changed my life. They have thought simply when I was overthinking. They have trusted God like small children when I was thinking like a foolish adult.

So do I, as lead pastor, submit to others? Yes. I'm the founding pastor of Real Life Ministries, and any founding or lead pastor needs to be a hard charger. But the Bible still calls me to submit—to be accountable. In fact, one of the first things a leader needs to do is to form a spiritual accountability relationship with other mature people in the church. A person without accountability is in a dangerous place, and so are the people they lead.

Submitting to Wise Counsel

A few years back, some of my elders asked me to work on an area of my life they felt needed some attention. They felt I wasn't listening to them enough and had fallen into a pattern of seeking to convince rather than listening. When I disagreed with them, they felt like I was cutting them off and not considering their opinions highly enough.

The overall specific problem was that I wanted to keep expanding the church by going through doors I felt God had opened. I felt we had begun to manage rather than to lead into areas where we could reach more lost people. I did not take their point of view very well. I was frustrated and didn't want to hear it, so I began to contemplate whether it was time to leave, to begin something new somewhere else.

But as I talked with my spiritual counselors on the eldership and friends on staff, they began to challenge my thinking. Added to this, on a trip to India, I spent time with a leader named K.P. Yohannon. As I shared my thoughts, he asked me to read a book he had written (*Touching Godliness*). The book challenged me in ways that I had not considered before, and it lined up perfectly with what my spiritual counselors in my church were saying. Several of these counselors had asked me the same question the book had addressed (which is usually a sign God is speaking). They asked if I believed God speaks through the leadership team. They knew the answer but wanted me to say it out loud. They asked me to reaffirm that, even for a leader, humility is a characteristic of a mature believer. They asked if the elders had asked me to do something contrary to the Word or just contrary to my plan.

As I began to pray about all of this and let others speak into my life, I knew what I needed to do: submit to the authority of the plurality of elders. As I prayed for help, I began to really try to hear what they were saying. I realized that they were praying and wanted to do what God wanted. They believed we needed to slow our approach for a while so we could become more effective at discipling those we had already reached. They were concerned that we could become "a mile wide but an inch deep." We could still grow, they said, but we needed to grow effectively and according to the Spirit's leading, not simply explosively.

As it pertains to the way I was responding to their challenges to my plan, they were not feeling like I was listening well. They felt I was not showing them the love I said I had for them when I reacted by answering back quickly and intensely rather than patiently. Again, the elders weren't asking me to do something unbiblical. They were asking me to do something wise and kind. When I approached those who were my wise counsel, they also challenged me to think about how I had responded to those who had left the church over the years—those I had rightly challenged when they told me they had been led by God to leave but the real issue was petty and unbiblical. They asked me to think about whether I was potentially doing the same thing if I were to leave simply because I did not agree with the elders' decision.

In the end I accepted the elders' decision to change our emphasis for a season. I also told them that I heard their concerns about my attitude as a leader. I told them that if this direction was the way they prayerfully believed the Lord was leading, then I wanted to submit to their authority. Leadership comes with potential temptations that can lead a person to destruction. It is also a responsibility that comes with accountability. I didn't want to be a dictator. See, God wanted me to *be* something before He wanted me to *do* something. God wanted me to be in relationship with these elders. He wanted me to love and be loved, to know and be known.

A Christian leader (paid or volunteer) must realize that the job is a privilege and a responsibility. It's not a privilege in the sense that they get to use it to merely meet their own need for a living and a position of influence. It is a privilege in the sense that we get to be involved in something eternal when we do not deserve it. We get to be used by God and we get to see the miracles He can do firsthand. We must remember, however, that leadership comes with a warning. Few should be teachers and preachers because they will incur a stricter judgment (James 3:1). Leadership is a responsibility that comes with accountability. Leaders must not lord their positions over other people. They are not the voice of God alone to their churches; they may hear from the Lord, but godly leaders will confirm God's plan through the Word and through a plurality of praying leaders. Leadership is about laying down your life for others. According to Ezekiel 34, our job as leaders is to care for people, to seek people who have gone astray, to help bring healing to those who are hurt, and to ensure that those under us receive good, biblical feeding. That's not the description of a dictator. That's the description of a wise, godly, strong, and compassionate shepherd.

Whether or not we are leaders, James 3:13–18 continually pulls us toward wisdom, peacefulness, and humility.

> Who is wise and understanding among you? Let them show it by their good life, by deeds done in the humility that comes from wisdom. But if you harbor bitter envy and selfish ambition in your hearts, do not boast about it or deny the truth. Such "wisdom" does not come down from heaven

but is earthly, unspiritual, demonic. For where you have envy and selfish ambition, there you find disorder and every evil practice.

But the wisdom that comes from heaven is first of all pure; then peace-loving, considerate, submissive, full of mercy and good fruit, impartial and sincere. Peacemakers who sow in peace reap a harvest of righteousness.

There is that concept again—submission. So many Christians think they are wise, but by James's description of wisdom, they miss the mark. They are not under the authority of any human they don't want to be under. If we are not under the authority of anyone unless they agree with us, then are we really under anyone's authority at all?

Finding Courage to Be Humble

Do we know what true humility is? Can we point to examples in ourselves and in other believers?

True humility doesn't mean we become doormats. It doesn't mean we acquiesce to every opinion or direction from others. With true humility, we're entitled to opinions and preferences of our own.

True humility involves courage. It's easy to go our own way when people don't see it the way we do. But with humility, we courageously stick around and work things out. We seek to understand and be understood. We don't come into a disagreement waving a big stick, insistent that we are the only one right. We listen. We consider other people's viewpoints. We realize that we can be misunderstood and may need to repeat ourselves or describe an issue a different way. Sometimes others are wiser than we are in a given area, and this shouldn't threaten us. We should be grateful that the responsibility for spiritual direction isn't just on our shoulders—it's given to a group that prays for God's will together.

With true humility, we allow others to speak into our lives. We realize that God can speak to us through others; that's part of the whole counsel of God, as long as the words people speak align with Scripture.

What should you do at your church when things don't go the way you want? Start with prayer. The church body is your family. You wouldn't walk away from your family, would you, for just any disagreement or misunderstanding? No. You give grace to your family members. You don't take off after an argument and divorce your family. You work things through because divorce is not an option. You are okay if things don't always go your way.

So many verses in the Bible have to do with establishing and keeping loving commitments within the body of Christ.

Galatians 6:10 says, "Therefore, as we have opportunity, let us do good to all people, especially to those who belong to the family of believers." This verse sets the tone for so many other passages. The commandment to love others applies to all people, but it especially applies to other Christians.

Galatians 6:2 tells us to "bear each other's burdens" (NASB). That means we listen to each other when things aren't going smoothly. We pray for people. We love them through difficulties. We don't simply take off when the going gets rough.

Ephesians 4:32 tells us to "be kind and compassionate to one another, forgiving each other, just as in Christ God forgave you." We will disagree with one another, yes. But the key is to keep being kind and compassionate, even in the midst

128

of disagreements. If someone wrongs us, we are to forgive, and if we wrong someone, they are to forgive, all of us continually working toward harmony, peace, and reconciliation. Romans 12:18 says, "If it is possible, as far as it depends on you, live at peace with everyone." Sometimes we encounter people who do not want to get along with us. Sometimes a disagreement genuinely will be the other person's fault. But our task is to do whatever we can to reconcile a relationship, as far as it depends on us. Hebrews 12:14 says, "Make every effort to live in peace with everyone and to be holy; without holiness no one will see the Lord." That's a powerful verse.

Proverbs 19:11 says, "A person's wisdom yields patience; it is to one's glory to overlook an offense." That means it's just good, plain sense to be slow to become angry. Typically, it's far, far better to overlook an offense.

Philippians 2:4 encourages us to "not [be] looking to your own interests but each of you to the interests of the others." This promotes true empathy, putting ourselves in another's shoes. What perspective does another person bring to the table? Can we see an issue through someone else's eyes?

I love Psalm 133:1: "How good and pleasant it is when God's people live together in unity!" That pretty much sums it all up. The psalmist acknowledges the beauty of true fellowship, of doing life together, of growing into true spiritual maturity, a maturity that comes from right relationships.

The Responsibility to Remain Committed

As Christians, what is our responsibility to our pastors, elders, and spiritual leaders in our church? Hebrews 13:17 lays it out plainly: "Have confidence in your leaders and submit to their authority, because they keep watch over you as those who must give an account. Do this so that their work will be a joy, not a burden, for that would be of no benefit to you." I've quoted that verse from the NIV, but the phrase "have confidence in your leaders" is, I believe, rendered a bit too soft in that translation. In Greek, the phrase is *peithesthe tois hēgoumenois humōn*, and a better translation is "continue to obey your leaders." How does that sit in your soul? Have you "obeyed" your pastor lately as he brings the Word of God into your life?

We Christians sometimes believe our job is to continually evaluate and critique our pastors. If he passes the test we give him in our head, we will continue to go to church there. If he preaches a sermon about vision and asks us to get involved, we will stay if we like what he asks us to get involved in. If he asks Christians to give, we shrug that off unless we like what the church does with the money. (I am not saying we should give to a church that embezzles money for a pastor's comfort and so on. But most churches I know of use money for godly reasons.) If a sermon isn't up to par in presentation, we let our pastor know. If attendance at church is down, we wonder if it's time for a new pastor. If a program doesn't go smoothly, we blame our pastor for not being organized. If someone we know strays from the faith, we expect the pastor to bring that person back.

But Hebrews 13:17 points us in a different direction. We are to submit to our leaders' authority "so that their work will be a joy, not a burden, for that would be of no benefit to [us]." The principle here is that it's actually in our best interest *not* to criticize our pastors or outright disobey what they teach about how a biblical Christian should behave. When pastors are continually criticized, they typically become defensive or discouraged—they do their job worse, not better—and that doesn't benefit anybody, including us. So often pastors are in a spiritual battle for their own homes and for the lives of people in the church, and a critical spirit from one they serve can just reinforce what the devil has already been whispering in their ear. But when we support and submit to our pastors' authority, life is actually smoother for us. We can encourage our leaders and glorify God by using our gifts when we see the need or opportunity.

Christians are responsible to be committed to both their pastor and their church. It's far too easy to criticize a pastor or church while forgetting how much good that pastor or church has done in their lives or in their family.

Years ago in my home group, we walked through long-standing issues with one couple. We helped them with their marriage and parenting. We helped them move twice. We helped them financially (all of those in the home group had contributed). After their lives became more stable, they missed a few weeks of home group and church, so I called and asked them if they were okay.

"Oh, we got invited to another church with some friends," the man said. "We like how small it is, and they were going through the book of Revelation and we are really interested. So we're going to go to the other church from now on, but we will stop in and see you every once in a while."

I couldn't believe it. Was our church too big when their child ran away and we all gathered to search for him? Was it too big when my wife and I went to their house at midnight to help them work through a marriage fight? Was our church too big when our home group helped them by bringing meals when one of them was in the hospital? And the time we all worked on their house because they couldn't afford renovations? And my noticing that they were gone from home group and church and caring enough to phone and ask if everything was okay?

At that point, it usually does no good to remind someone of the support and relationships they had. The common response is, "All we did was change churches. We'll visit sometime. Don't take it personally."

"But it is personal," I would say. "It's personal because we're family. Would you tell me it wasn't personal if you were my son and were leaving me for another father? Is it personal when a husband leaves his wife for another woman? You may think this goes too far, but show me that in Scripture. Show me where we have the right to bounce from church to church, never really being committed."

So many believers think the church's obligation is to be there for them—a one-way street. The pastor needs to study so he can preach a sermon that deals with their real issues. Leaders in the church need to visit them in the hospital. The pastor must officiate the wedding when their kids get married. The weekend services should be organized and helpful to the whole family.

But do believers have an equal obligation to the church?

Relationship is a two-way street. God wants to make us secure and strong through a form of relationship that entails mutual submission. Relationships are like ropes, binding us to other people. As a spiritual family, we develop ties, and those ties are not easily broken. They *shouldn't* be easy to break. We have a responsibility to be committed to one another. If a family down the street looks better than ours, we don't just leave our family and head down to the other house to eat dinner every night. Of course, the other family may look perfect, but make no bones about it—it has its problems too. You just don't see them yet because you don't eat and live with them every day. Besides, much of the problem in your family may be you, and if you join theirs, you end up bringing your baggage with you. We need to fight to keep relationships intact. If something is missing in the family we are a part of, then we do all we can to allow God to use us to bring in the ingredient that will make it better. We don't just tell the leader what it should look like; we ask how we can invest in the solution.

Certainly, I'm not advocating some sort of cultlike system where we never question those in authority over us or never leave for any reason. I'm not advocating blind allegiance. Rather, I'm advocating biblical allegiance. There's a big difference. If a church is ungodly, then it's okay to leave, but only after you have done everything a wise believer can do to make things right. If a pastor is teaching heresy, go somewhere else. But there is a biblical approach to this—it's found in Matthew 18, where Jesus addresses relationships and the church.

> If your brother or sister sins, go and point out their fault, just between the two of you. If they listen to you, you have won them over. But if they will not listen, take one or two others along, so that "every matter may be established by the testimony of two or three witnesses." If they still refuse to listen, tell it to the church; and if they refuse to listen even to the church, treat them as you would a pagan or a tax collector. (Matt. 18:15–17)

Notice Jesus makes it clear that we approach them in private first. We seek to make things right between us if there is a disagreement. If someone is caught in a sin, we seek to point it out to them in humility and kindness because we love them. We try to resolve it courageously and humbly before we go. Leaving should be the last resort, and we need to ask God about our own attitude as we think through this.

The Only Way Forward

What will you do about submitting? Will you continue to be a "spiritually democratic" Christian, always voting with your feet? I call this immature Christianity. Or will you forbear with one another and submit to one another out of love?

One final thought: Christians are called to be disciple-makers, people who go out into the world and make other disciples. This principle is laid out in the Great Commission, Matthew 28:18–20:

> [Jesus] said, "All authority in heaven and on earth has been given to me. Therefore go and make disciples of all nations, baptizing them in the name of the Father and of the Son and of the Holy Spirit, and teaching them to obey everything I have commanded you. And surely I am with you always, to the very end of the age."

The process of being disciple-makers implies that somebody is being discipled. And to be discipled, we must be under spiritual authority to someone else. Real discipleship happens in relationship, and to be a disciple implies submission in that relationship. As I wrote earlier, it makes sense that we learn to be relational in relationship. But it also makes sense that we learn to be surrendered and submitted to the Lord by being in submission to those who disciple us.

If we allow God's Word to guide both the person making the disciple and the one who is being discipled, we can avoid the pitfalls of spiritual abuse. God calls us to follow our leaders as they follow Christ. Jesus is the perfect example of a submissive follower of God who exemplified humility and strength. He is also the perfect example of spiritual leadership. He told the truth in love and did not abuse His power.

It's time for us as believers to stop voting with our feet. It's time for us to be people who are characterized by relationship. Love by its very nature is submissive. It is to lay down your life for the good of others. Ephesians 5:22 and the verses following tell us that a wife submits to her husband as to the Lord. The husband gives himself up for his wife. Children obey their parents. Christians obey their leaders in the church, the workplace, and the government. We all obey Jesus and all He has to say about life and faith. When we live in submission to God, we are able to enjoy the benefits of relationship that come as a result. God's call on our lives is to bear with one another and to submit to one another out of love. As the family of God, we can't be healthy without it. We are called to join a church because we *are* the church. Then we're called to stick with that one church through thick and thin. We are called to commit to that church for better or worse. We don't leave simply if things get difficult. We don't attend another church for six weeks while our pastor preaches on tithing because we don't like that subject. We don't jump around from church to church, shopping for the best "experience."

We stick with our family.

Because that's what family does.

7

A Better Return for Our Labor

Let's review. If you are like me, you read a bit and then put the book down for a while. Later on you start again and some of what you read has lost its context and meaning. So let me remind you of our foundational principle: We are created in the image of God to be in relationship. We are designed with relationship in mind.

God is a relational God and always has been. The Trinity has existed forever in a loving, purposeful relationship, and God asks us to join Him in that relationship. We lost our ability to have what we were designed for because we all chose to sin, but God has been seeking to reconcile us to relationship with Him and has given us the ministry of reconciliation. A group of reconcilers should, by the way, be reconciled to one another if they are practicing the habit of reconciliation.

As we walk with Him in the light, God gives us the ability to be in fellowship with one another (1 John 1:5–7). But it's not just about us having relationship for relationship's sake. It's so we can together do the work God has given us as individuals and as a church.

One of my favorite New Testament passages concerning this is familiar, but often the point is missed: "For we are God's masterpiece. He has created us anew in Christ Jesus, so we can do the good things he planned for us long ago" (Eph. 2:10 NLT). This tells us that we (plural), the body of Christ, are God's "masterpiece" (*handiwork* in the NIV). We may think this is speaking about the individual Christian, but notice the context. While it is true that God is in the process of restoring the individual to become the masterpiece He purposed, and He does have work for individuals that has been in His plan from before time began, the point of this passage is even larger.

This verse is written to the Ephesian church as a whole. Paul will later tell us that we are the body of Christ. We are under the Head (Jesus). And we are to grow into maturity as the body of Christ, which means we join together and become mature, a team. Just as Paul in every letter has written of the importance of being the body of Christ working together, he does it again here. Yes, some work we can only do as individual Christians, such as sharing faith with a friend. But other work can be accomplished only together as the family of God. Paul is telling us that we (the church) are a masterpiece when we share the load and work together.

Poured Out and Poured Into

A foundational passage that points to the need for togetherness in our work is Ecclesiastes 4:8–12. We've looked at part of this passage before, but I want us to look at the longer portion in the context of our labor and service for Christ.

> There was a man all alone;
>> he had neither son nor brother.
> There was no end to his toil,
>> yet his eyes were not content with his wealth.
> "For whom am I toiling," he asked,
>> "and why am I depriving myself of enjoyment?"
> This too is meaningless—
>> a miserable business!
>
> Two are better than one,
>> because they have a good return for their labor:
> If either of them falls down,
>> one can help the other up.
> But pity anyone who falls
>> and has no one to help them up.
> Also, if two lie down together, they will keep warm.
>> But how can one keep warm alone?
> Though one may be overpowered,
>> two can defend themselves.
> A cord of three strands is not quickly broken.

The passage paints a picture of a man doing his best to work alone. He's without family or friend, and all he does is work, work, work. He's apparently got plenty to do, and one result of all his hard work is that he's grown wealthy. But his work lacks meaning and he's unhappy. He's unclear about why he is working so hard—he's got no one to share his wealth with.

This was written more than three thousand years ago, but it accurately describes the modern man who's trying to make it to the top. He's made some poor choices along the way that have left him alone. In the end, he's miserable and depressed. He might own the amazing house and the expensive car, but there is no one in the house or car with him. He's certainly not satisfied.

This passage reflects many of today's Christians and even leaders. Some have no problem serving others, but let someone into their heart? No thank you. Yes, we are to serve people, but we also serve with them. This gets the work done better, and a work is also done in our own hearts too. When we serve, we are being poured *out for sure*, but God's plan was to continually pour into us so there is always something to pour out of us. God works through others in our lives, and through His people He pours into us what we need to live and serve. Those who attempt to serve alone, even for a good cause, eventually burn out or develop a calloused and bitter heart, and the greater work of discipling those who can disciple others is thwarted.

The person serving alone might be a senior pastor who doesn't think anyone else is available, capable, educated, committed, or loving enough—so he doesn't ask for help. He might be tempted to believe his importance is tied to his ability and position, so he is threatened by anyone who might learn to do what he does. He might believe that he cannot trust anyone to hear his inner spiritual struggle, so he pours out his heart to Jesus only and keeps others at a distance.

When the church leader functions this way, people often follow his example. So a ministry leader or a home group leader will try to shoulder the responsibilities of the group or project alone. It might be a worship team member who never takes a Sunday off because he believes his position is indispensable and no one can play the drums like he can. Or even a Christian blogger who fails to enlist the prayer support of her home group.

Christians have plenty of Christ-honoring work to do, for sure. But unless we see our work and ministries as something we must do together, we're on a fast track to burnout, misery, depression, and failure. Unless we work and minister with the truth of Ecclesiastes 4:9 ringing loudly in our ears ("Two are better than one, because they have a good return for their labor"), our work will become an empty experience. According to the Ecclesiastes passage, we are in danger of being discontented, overpowered, defenseless, and joyless.

Fortunately, the solution is clearly pointed out in Ecclesiastes. The solution is relationships. Work is better and there is a better outcome when it's shared with others. Without relationships, something will be missing in our lives. Philippians 1:27 says, "Stand firm in the one Spirit, striving together as one for the faith of the gospel."

That means we must intentionally decide to make it a priority to work in and through relationships. Spiritually mature people make these choices. They often must choose to do fewer things in their lives so what they do take on they can do well, and together in relationship. In my younger years, we could only afford one tank of gas a week, and this forced my wife and me to make decisions about where we would go and what we would do. We eliminated many unnecessary trips just so our gas would last the week. In the same way, there are only so many hours available to all of us, and so often we spend them in ways that do not really help us achieve the most important things. So often the good things can keep us from the best things. When we choose to do the best things together with others, it takes more time than we think. Working with others isn't easy. We are people with sinful natures—our spiritual enemy seeks to stop the work of God by dividing us. We have different filters for hearing and different skill sets that can get us working at odds unless we intentionally focus on unity and love. These choices lead to a Christian experience that's designed by God to be all it can be.

Make Teamwork a Priority

I can hear you contemplating the problems.

You might be saying the pastor of your church is a one-man show. He wouldn't let you serve. You know because you've tried.

You might be thinking about how you've attempted to work with other believers but you didn't agree on anything, let alone on what you felt the Lord had put on your heart.

Or you might be remembering you've been hurt by others and you don't want to let people in again.

As a Christian leader, you might be thinking that plenty of people in your church aren't, in your mind, ready to do any sort of Christian service. You've got broken, hurting, immature people who seem in no position to help out in any way. It's hard for them to even be friends with others, much less work well with others. They've been so wounded that they can hardly take any kind of direction at all because they mistake it for criticism.

Or they're prideful, arrogant, bossy, inflexible control freaks. They can't handle their ideas being tweaked because they only hear—mistakenly—"You're bad." What do you do with these people? Where do you start?

I get that. Many Christians simply want to be affirmed, not coached. Others have worked alone for so long that they have become lone rangers and don't know how to be on a team. As I wrote earlier, to them the word *submission* is bad. The devil has had his way with the body of Christ for a long time, so it takes work to become a team again. No matter what role you are in, the solution starts with the affirmation that God's church is supposed to be a team and you and everyone else are supposed to play your parts.

If you recognize that you have not been part of a team, then it's time to start praying and ask God and yourself why. Repentance must play a part in the change. To repent means you recognize that it has been wrong to be out of relationship with others. It means that you have a change of heart that leads to a change of action. Then it's time to join a team. Or if you are leading something within the church but not leading it like a spiritual team, then it's time to make some changes. There is plenty of ministry to be done. If your pastor has not led you into teamwork, remember that he still has spiritual authority and you should ask him if you can help. You might give him this book and begin to pray for him. If he is open to giving you ministry opportunities, then begin to think about developing a team to meet the needs. Remember that the team not only meets the needs of others; it also meets the relational needs of those on the team. Be honest and share with your potential team that you're new at this and perhaps do not know how to do it very well and will make mistakes.

Ask for grace, and when (not if) you make a mistake, don't be defensive—listen to and pray about what others say to you.

Don't allow the ministry tasks to take over the group. Begin to do life with those on the team. Pray together. Have dinner together. Have fun together. Go camping or to a park. Spend the first part of every gathering abiding in Christ. This means you read Scripture together and share your struggles and pray for one another, then begin the ministry task. When you serve, don't do it alone; take someone with you.

When you get a ministry goal accomplished, celebrate together; allow people to rest together spiritually and have some fun. Thank those who stepped out. When someone tries something for the first time, celebrate that they tried, whether or not it was perfect. Only by trying and sometimes failing do we get better at the doing. Courage to try leads to excellence later on, so celebrate courage and trying your best. Celebrate humility when someone accepts coaching and makes changes. Lead the way by asking others to share with you as the leader how you could have done it more effectively.

Build relational bank accounts that have more in them than you will need to spend. As a developing coach, you will need to confront in love at times. If your people know you love them and you have said many more uplifting and supportive things to them than the occasional challenging or confrontational thing, then they will hear you when you must tweak their attempts.

If you have people who need to be encouraged to minister but they're not yet ready for it, begin by getting them into relationship with mature believers so they can do the task together. A good leader always debriefs the shared ministry opportunities after they are done. They celebrate the good things and the effort, and they unpack the things that could be done better next time, starting with their own role first.

Let them see and feel what spiritual maturity looks like. Bring them along slowly. Cast the vision of being a disciple of Jesus who makes other disciples. Remind them that Jesus's disciples failed many times, but Jesus picked them up, dusted them off, and sent them right back onto the field. Don't simply throw this vision down in front of them; let them buy into it on their own. This happens when they get to hear the why behind the chosen activity and they are able to play a part in the how, as the team plans together. Then gradually hand them more and more responsibility while directing and affirming.

Working toward the Goal

At Real Life Ministries, we regularly hold seminars to train people in our discipleship processes and methodology. Pastors bring their whole church staffs and volunteer leadership to go through the two-day experience. Intentionally, we keep the up-front teaching by one person or persons down to a minimum so people can experience discipleship in and through relationship in groups. The groups are led by a combination of our staff and volunteers in our church. We do this because we want the students to see how discipleship happens best in relationship rather than just hearing about it. In a sense, we are also discipling volunteers in front of pastors so they can see how it is done. We also have about thirty volunteers putting together the meals and dealing with the details in every facet of our time together.

Afterward, we debrief with the attendees about their take-aways from their journey with us. The most common thing we hear might surprise you—it surprised us at first. They make comments like, "Wow, it blows us away how well your folks work as a team and even more so how much you guys really love each other." They often then ask if the teamwork is only a show or if it works like this all the time at Real Life. I share that it really is this way but not all the time, as we have had many battles to resolve differences of opinion and even bad attitudes. I share how hard we have had to work for smooth teamwork and real relationship to result. We often receive notes afterward from attendees expressing their desire for such relationships. Leaders often commend us on our teamwork, because they wish they had the same sort of teamwork in their churches.

But here's reality: At Real Life Ministries, we work well as teams only because we work hard at being teams. Did you catch that? We prioritize teamwork and relationship. We put time and energy into functioning as a team, and because of that prioritization, most of our teams eventually succeed. We have a lot of solid, high-functioning leaders today because we choose to work together and resolve differences.

Another comment we often hear is that we are so blessed to have great leaders at our church. But I answer, "How do you think they got to be good leaders? We followed the mandates that are right there in Scripture, and the Holy Spirit always empowers what He directs through Scripture. Our people got a chance to be on a team. As they played on the team, they got better at their individual positions. Because they were coached and because they listened, they were helped up when they failed or struggled. No one gets great at something without some great failures. They were listened to when plans were made. They were encouraged to listen to others. We have good leaders because we made true spiritual maturity a priority." By now I hope you know that I don't think someone is mature merely because they do a task well. Maturity is to love God and others well and to become great at relationship.

Does this mean every leader is always mature? No. How could that possibly be true when we are such broken people and have such a spiritual enemy? Life down here is a fight until Jesus returns, so the question isn't whether or not there is a fight; it's whether we are fighting the right fight in the right way.

Spiritually immature Christians can become prideful and keep their work to themselves. Even spiritually mature people can forget who they are and slip back into immaturity. This creates silos in the church (the larger team), and the lack of teamwork means less effectiveness and a less unified team handling the whole scope of work. As individuals, when we don't allow our thoughts to be challenged or tweaked, we are often like an unsharpened axe. We work hard but get little done. This can lead to discouragement, exhaustion, and ultimately to quitting. When we don't listen to other people or solicit their input, we end up only with our own viewpoint. Many times our own perspective can oversimplify or overcomplicate things. Even if we intend to give God glory through our work, if we go it alone we tend to allow people to give us the credit rather than give it to God.

Pride can destroy a person who takes the glory. It gives the enemy an opportunity to puff them up and make them too important in their own eyes. The devil knows that God opposes the proud and gives grace to the humble so if he can get a person to become the point rather than the tool God uses, God will not only stop blessing the work but may even come against it.

A Fuller, Wiser Counsel

When I write about a better return for our labor, I don't just mean that many hands lead to less and better work in a physical sense. I also mean that with many eyes, minds, talents, and spiritual giftings and insights a better plan is formed before we actually start the work.

I wish I had known this before I needed to learn it the hard way. I have learned the benefit of teams and wise counsel through many failures. We planted Real Life Ministries more than fifteen years ago, and in a small growing church you never seem to have enough staff—you can't afford it. Everybody on staff must wear multiple hats, and every volunteer works on several teams. During those first few years, I was constantly stressed out, always running around trying to do all I could to keep our new young church afloat.

One of the things that stressed me the most was sermon preparation. It just took me so much time. And even when I preached a good sermon, sometimes I'd have people coming to me afterward telling me that I missed out on important things that could have made it better. Now, I admit that I was emphasizing my own ability rather than allowing the Holy Spirit to do His work. I also understand that some people put too much pressure on me to be perfect, and I allowed it. But there was a way to do a better job that I had not discovered yet. The result was that I missed things, making more work that could have been avoided.

For instance, one year during the Christmas season I preached on the real reason for Christmas during our Christmas Eve services. Of course we had many first-timers because I had encouraged our people to invite unsaved friends and family. We did not have our children's ministry open that night, so there were a ton of young children sitting with their parents. During the service I made the point that Christmas isn't about Santa Claus—in fact, Santa Claus isn't even real. Christmas is about a true story, I proclaimed—Jesus in a manger, God with us.

That's when problems began. I noticed that a bunch of parents with young children put their hands over their kids' ears. I saw some little heads turn toward their shocked parents, already asking if it was true, that Santa wasn't real. I saw angry parent faces looking at me. A few families even walked out. See, I'd made the classic mistake of forgetting to take into account the context I was preaching in. I could have put myself in the visitors' shoes. Way to burst their bubble! Of course there is no Santa Claus, but I could have worded that portion of my sermon differently to be more sensitive. What made matters worse was that when I got home my wife asked in front of my whole family if I was going to kill the Easter Bunny at Easter.

Another time I was preaching on the family, and I was talking about the differences between men and women. I made the comment in the form of a joke that men just don't understand women and it can cause huge problems. All the guys in the audience laughed. But our women's minister came to me later and gently said, "You know what your female listeners might have construed from your sermon? That the senior pastor doesn't understand women and doesn't really care to, so our husbands don't need to understand us either." For some of the men who are immature, she said, they would use my words as an excuse to continue their uncaring behavior. She shared how many women she worked with felt their husbands were not who God wants them to be and how much it hurts the family. Well, that's not what I intended at all. I was just trying to add some levity to an intense subject. But to some it had come across badly. Honestly, I so wished I had thought of that angle before I said it, but it was too late.

Sermon preparation was eating up all my time. I spent between twenty and thirty hours each week just on sermon prep and, quite honestly, still missed the mark. That was on top of the thirty to forty or so other hours I spent in other church-related work. I was running myself ragged. This was not a healthy Christian life, and it was affecting my marriage, my parenting, and my ability to be a good spiritual leader.

I talked to an older pastor about what to do. He had planted a church many years before, and he told me about something he designed in his church called "Sermon Club." He brought in a bunch of staff members and laypeople for a meeting early in the week to collaborate on the sermon. It was a way to get outside his own perspective.

So I tried it. As I began to do this, I found that in one hour I was getting about fifteen hours' worth of work done. I was able to try out some of my thoughts and ideas on a group that could tell me what they heard. (This would have been nice to do before the Christmas Eve debacle.) They gave me input that I had not thought about and helped me apply principles. The women in the group gave me better ways to relate to women.

Younger staff gave me better illustrations that could touch the hearts of the young. My older, wiser staff gave me input into how the Greek or Hebrew might be used and offered a more expanded interpretation. Our volunteers who attended gave me some thoughts about how the message would apply to the business owner or the employee of a bank and so on.

Sermon Club gave me a faster way to study and a better way to relate to others. By working as a team, I was getting wise counsel and a broader perspective than my own. This freed up time for me to do all that I needed to do as a leader and to be balanced at home.

I discovered other benefits as well. My staff saw that if I could work with others, so could they. If I could seek wise counsel, so could they. It also helped them start to understand how to develop lessons, and this accelerated their growth process in communicating. I developed speakers even as I developed sermons.

For years now I've done Sermon Club each week and it's worked really well. Not long ago I brought a new guy on staff. He came from another church, so he had a completely different view of how you develop a message. He came to Sermon Club as part of the team, and I could tell that about the third time he came, he was very frustrated. I talked with him afterward.

"What's bothering you?" I said.

"You're the pastor, Jim," he said. "God speaks to you. But these people come to the club and don't support what you believe about how the sermon should go. They even challenge it. Who do they think they are? They're always asking questions. 'What about this? What about that?' Your sermons don't end up the way you wanted at first. That makes me frustrated."

"Let me help you understand the vision," I said. "If you think that God speaks to me alone, and that everybody else in the church only exists to fulfill my mission, then you have the wrong perspective of how God speaks. God may put something on my heart, but that message is confirmed and thought through and lived out as a church body. Too many pastors believe that their sermons are the voice of God flowing directly from God through them alone to their congregations. I also believe that too many pastors think it's their job to get a vision from God and then to tell it to their churches. I agree that God can give a leader a vision, but He works out that vision through the body of believers He has placed the leader in. We've got to allow other mature believers to be involved in the process. Certainly God puts things on our hearts, but the Scriptures tell us to seek wise counsel. God's Word, God's Spirit, and God's people all work together to give us direction."

I could tell he was really trying to get his mind around what I was saying, so I added, "Look—you're super effective at what you do. But if you think it's your job as a pastor to tell everybody else what to do, then you need to know that it's not. It's your job to listen, facilitate, coach, and to be a disciple of Jesus who makes other disciples and other disciple-makers. Lead from your position as a team member. Work well with other disciples. Value the other people on the team."

I realize that not every pastor in North America will start a Sermon Club tomorrow, but it's one way to practice the principle of doing things together. A pastor might run each sermon by a few key individuals, or enlist prayer support from his home group, or maintain an open spirit to receiving input, particularly as he does life together with others. The point is that our labor is always better accomplished as a team. God puts wise people into our lives, and when we solicit their input, it gives us fuller perspectives. If I choose to work alone, all my communications will be filtered solely through my experiences and my education and my exegesis. My work will emerge narrower than I think God desires. But God has given us the body of Christ to help us see things in a fuller way.

Paul points us to true humility, to living in light of Christ's example. Paul acknowledges that we don't all have the same individual function, but all the gifts are given for the same purpose: to glorify God, make disciples, and build up other believers in the faith. Romans 12:3–8 says,

> For by the grace given me I say to every one of you: Do not think of yourself more highly than you ought, but rather think of yourself with sober judgment, in accordance with the faith God has distributed to each of you. For just as each of us has one body with many members, and these members do not all have the same function, so in Christ we, though many, form one body, and each member belongs to all the others. We have different gifts, according to the grace given to each of us. If your gift is prophesying, then prophesy in accordance with your faith; if it is serving, then serve; if it is teaching, then teach; if it is to encourage, then give encouragement; if it is giving, then give generously; if it is to lead, do it diligently; if it is to show mercy, do it cheerfully.

In Ephesians 4:11, Paul points out the leadership giftings that help direct the affairs of the body of Christ and call the church to action:

> Christ himself gave the apostles, the prophets, the evangelists, the pastors and teachers.

In 1 Corinthians 1:10 Paul urges Christians not to be divided, but for the church to use the diversity of gifting to function as a single entity, united in purpose and practice. In our modern culture, we would see this as team language. Unless the team unites in its goal and the method to attain it, the amount of talent doesn't matter.

> I appeal to you, brothers and sisters, in the name of our Lord Jesus Christ, that all of you agree with one another in what you say and that there be no divisions among you, but that you be perfectly united in mind and thought.

In 1 Corinthians 12 Paul acknowledges the incredible diversity in the body while continually pointing believers to unity under the leadership of Christ.

> Just as a body, though one, has many parts, but all its many parts form one body, so it is with Christ. (v. 12)

The point is that only when we come together is the wisdom of God revealed. His plan is amazing when it works as He intended it to. Not only do we get much more and better work done but we find the answer to our relational issues as we experience the joy and strength that comes from doing life together.

The Whole Measure of Fullness

Let me offer a specific word to leaders. In Ephesians 4:12–13 Paul is clear that our job is to "equip [God's] people for works of service, so that the body of Christ may be built up until we all reach unity in the faith and in the knowledge of the Son of God and become mature, attaining to the whole measure of the fullness of Christ."

This biblical principle sounds so basic, but many leaders fail to grasp it. Our job is not to become superstars or to have the spotlight shined on us. We are not the paid players; we are called to be the coaches. Our job is to get others into the game. Our job is not just to tell others what to do, it's to provide them with tools that equip them for service.

Imagine that you're a Little League coach. You're out coaching your team one day and the ball gets hit to the second baseman. What should he do? What's the job of the second baseman? Early on in your coaching sessions, you will need to tell the second baseman precisely what to do. You'll need to tell him to anticipate the line of the ball and move to where the ball will be. You'll coach him to get his glove ready and about how to catch the ball. You'll instruct him how to throw with power toward the first baseman so he can get the runner out. You'll walk him through it over and over until he becomes comfortable with his role on the field.

Now imagine you've been coaching your team for a while—the same players, the same scenario. The ball gets hit to the second baseman. What happens? The whole aim of coaching is that you get your player to the point where he knows exactly what to do without any more instruction. The training has set in. He knows exactly where to move, how to position his glove to catch the ball, and where to throw the ball to get the runner out. You've trained him to the point where he knows what to do and he's able to do it.

As leaders, that's our job in ministry too—training others so they know what to do and how to do it. But the problem is that in too many churches we've established a culture where the pastor is set up to fail. The pastor is seen as the star of the show. It's his job to do it all himself. He's taught that he's God's voice from heaven and His player for every position. His work is never done, and his work is all-consuming yet ill-defined, and everybody in the congregation looks to him to provide all the answers and do all the ministry. That type of environment is doomed from the start. We need to get our heads and hearts around the idea that there must be a plurality of leadership in a church, even if there's only one person called "pastor." The work of the ministry belongs to all Christians. It's the pastor's job to equip others so everyone is able to do the work of the ministry.

Not long ago we lost two of our main executive pastors at Real Life Ministries. They left for legitimate, God-honoring reasons, and the parting was positive. But we were left in a tough spot. I sat with the executive team in my office one afternoon and asked them what we were going to do. They gave me blank stares, and one finally said, "We don't know. We thought you were going to tell us what we should do."

"I don't have a clue what we should do," I said. "You're waiting for me to lead—and I will—but I'm looking to you for answers as part of the solution. Maybe one of you knows what we should do. Let's do it together. This is our problem as a team, and we need to tackle it as a team and overcome it as a team. So let's start from that perspective. The next move forward that we make will be made together."

One of the big reasons God designed us to work with other people as a team is that He gets credit for the success. Humans are designed to praise something, to thank somebody. Ultimately, humans are designed to give glory to God. When we as individuals perform well, the devil loves to pat us on the back so we'll get proud and territorial, and then we expect praise for our own accomplishments. Teamwork brings others in on the task and safeguards us from trying to take glory for ourselves. We know we are being filled with the Holy Spirit when we do something well and the glory goes to God instead of to us.

It seems like such a simple concept—working together—but it's one that consistently needs to be drilled into Christians. When we work together, our work has a better return. It's in our best interests to work as a team. Nowhere is this more important than in the church. In John 13:35, Jesus said, "By this everyone will know that you are my disciples, if you love one another." The church needs to present a unified front to the world. Not pretending but truly living it out behind the scenes. We need to get along with each other. God has commanded us to do so. He has given us the model to follow in Jesus and other mature believers in history. He has given us the Holy Spirit to enable us to obey. We, however, need to make it the priority it is supposed to be.

8

A Helping Hand

Not long ago, I called a man who had been missing from church for two weeks, and after several attempts, I reached him. I told him I'd missed him and asked if he was okay. He said he was fine, just busy. But something sounded different about his voice. I prodded him with more questions. Finally he broke. He told me things had been rough at work and the pressure was straining his marriage. He hadn't been at church for the last few weeks because he couldn't put on his "game face."

My heart went out to this man. Besides his other problems, he did not understand what authentic Christianity was really about. He thought he needed to act "fine" at church. Rather than seeing church as a place to be real and receive encouragement, he saw it as a place where he needed to, or at least appear to, have everything together. He had bought into the lie that a mature Christian needs to be perfect, and if not, people will judge him.

Another friend of mine had lost his job. He wasn't poor by global standards. He and his wife still had a roof over their heads and ate three meals a day. But they were broke. They were uncertain how to pay upcoming bills and stressed about their immediate and future financial situation.

He was a proud man, a longtime Christian, and he faced a decision. Should he tell people? He felt embarrassed and thought some would question his ability to manage money or to meet his family's needs. He had heard many sermons on hard work, stewardship, and laziness, so he believed others would see him as less than spiritually mature. He had been taught as a young man that "men don't whine"—when you fall down, you just rub some dirt on the wound, get up, and handle your business. He knew prayer could change things, so he really wanted prayer from his church, but he feared the prayer chain would become a launching pad for gossip. On one hand, he faced real need, but on the other, he was embarrassed to be one of "those" people—the ones who got the help rather than gave it.

In a different story, a woman who had been known as a servant began to be a no-show at the ministry where she had so faithfully served. For years she'd helped those who came to our church for food, and she walked them through the process of getting financial help. When she stopped coming around to serve, her friends pursued her to find out what was going on. When they finally caught up with her, she shared that she felt like she had nothing to give anymore because things had gotten tough at home with her husband and children. She felt her role was to help others, not to burden people with her problems.

Can you see yourself in any of those illustrations? There's a common denominator: People in need don't want to ask for help. They don't mind giving help, but asking? No way. That would mean they were less than they should be—even spiritually immature.

If you had a problem, would you tell people?

It's not just volunteers who fall into this trap. Many pastors I know are lonely for these same reasons. They care for others continually but refuse to trust others with their own insecurities, inner struggles, or even physical needs. Many pastors don't make much money, so they often have financial issues but won't share them. They have bought into the lie that a spiritually mature Christian has it all together and should be concerned only with serving others. No matter how life is going, they put on their game face and act as though life is just fine.

What does this teach the people they lead? It wrongly teaches that the church is a place where you serve and give and connect with God—and that's it. But the church is supposed to be a place where we also get encouragement and support from others.

Many think only the spiritually immature need help, while the spiritually mature do the helping. But mature Christians do both—they help when they are able, and they are also honest about their own needs because they know God blesses the humble. When we need help, God seldom answers our prayers by having us win the lottery or strike oil in our backyards like the Beverly Hillbillies. Instead, he answers prayers through other believers. It's actually the spiritually immature person who does not develop a spiritual family support system because he is too busy or too walled off emotionally. It's the immature person who will not communicate and will not let others love him by caring for his needs.

What sort of needs? Well, there are physical needs, such as shelter, gas, food, and clothing, and there are spiritual needs, such as prayer, encouragement, accountability, forgiveness, and wisdom. To have true relationships with people, we must initiate conversations that encourage those in our spiritual community to share their real needs. But we must also communicate our needs. We must have reciprocal, honest, and transparent relationships with people where *I know you* and *you know me*, and *I know what you need* and *you know what I need*.

How do we do this? And why?

Take the Risk

Many Christians have "friendly acquaintances," but they don't have real relationships. There's a difference. With acquaintances, we might golf or hunt, smile and shake hands. We might even be in a Bible study together or share certain prayer needs. But are we in the kind of relationship where we can be honest enough to share our deepest sin struggles? Do we allow ourselves to be known and helped when we need it? Are we really encouraging each other in the Lord when there is a tough marriage or work problem or parenting issue?

Look again at Ecclesiastes 4:9–11.

> Two are better than one,
>   because they have a good return for their labor:
> If either of them falls down,
>   one can help the other up.

But pity anyone who falls
and has no one to help them up.
Also, if two lie down together, they will keep warm.
But how can one keep warm alone?

Note verse 10: "If either of them falls down, one can help the other up." This points to the benefit of reciprocal togetherness. Help and understanding go both ways. If you and I are in true relationship, then I will know if you are straying close to the cliff before you step over the edge. It won't surprise me if there is a blowup in your house because of a long-term issue. You know what my potential weaknesses are, and you pray through them with me. You give me wise counsel about possible dangers. When I fall, you know it, because we are already communicating consistently.

Repeatedly, I deal with this kind of sad situation: A couple comes for counseling. They have been Christians for years. The marital struggle has gone on for a long time, but they've carried the burdens alone and they are exhausted and ready to give up. They haven't shared their problems with mature believers. Oftentimes they take advice from non-Christians or from far-removed television counselors or even from soap operas, and the counsel doesn't line up with God's plan. After trying everything else, they tell me I am the last hope, and if I can't help, they are done. They began falling a long time ago. Now, over time, hearts are hardened and emotional wounds are infected. Their spiritual lives are shallow, and we have a problem that I am not sure either of them has the spiritual strength or desire to do what it will take to fix.

You see, these people have concocted a recipe for an incomplete form of the faith. After a steady diet of it, they are empty and broken rather than strong and resolute. What is sad about couples like this is that often they have had friends along the way who would have listened and given godly counsel had they been honest. But whenever they were asked about their lives or marriage, they gave the old standby answer, "I am fine." Their spiritual friends would say they thought the couple was fine—but they weren't.

How did this happen? Often it's a lack of discipleship. Unfortunately, their spiritual community centered on events that lacked real relationships. Small groups and classes were about transfer of information only, but never unpacked real issues and methods that give a practical and powerful way to live through trials. The people may have helped others in a variety of ways but never let anyone into their real worlds. Their leaders may not have modeled authentic spirituality, so the people learned to always be fine as well. In fact, to "not be fine" was seen as weakness, an indication of spiritual immaturity.

Unfortunately, many Christians are continually in the role of giver or expert. This sounds noble, but it's actually a surefire ticket to struggle and disillusionment. It's also a subtle indication of pride. If I never communicate my needs to you, that hints I am above having problems. I might say I get my support from God, so I can always give to others, but this implies that God doesn't work through the others in my life. This implies that at an advanced stage of spiritual development I no longer need other believers to speak for God into my life. But authentic Christianity is incomplete without real relationships that strengthen and support.

When we don't live with relationships where we are known and know others, we sidetrack God's ability to deliver grace to us. If I have a physical problem, who will help me if I don't make that need known? Certainly God can perform miracles, yet He gave us language to communicate our needs to others so they can help us. He offers us His directions through His Word, which points us to humility so we can lay down our pride and admit we need help. If we have a spiritual problem, someone needs to walk this journey with us honestly. We need to establish a level of transparency in our relationships where both parties let down their guard.

Carrying Each Other's Burdens

Galatians 6:2 says, "Carry each other's burdens, and in this way you will fulfill the law of Christ." The law of Christ is all about relationships. What does it mean to carry each other's burdens? Obviously it means that we are to become servants of others as we become more like Christ, but it means more than that. It assumes I have developed real relationships with people who know me well enough to see I am struggling, and I allow them to help carry my burdens too. If others don't see it, I am not afraid to share so they can't miss it. This takes consistent and intentional time and effort. It means I have said no to many things that could take my time and energy so that I and others can have the best things.

This is why we work so hard in our church to help our people connect in home groups. We limit the church busyness so people have time to really connect outside of our reoccurring weekly worship service in our church building. We train our home group leaders to be transparent and honest so the people can learn what authentic relationship looks like. We urge our people not only to go to weekend services as God's Word directs us to, but to also meet in a smaller environment where deep relationships are built. But it doesn't stop there—these smaller groups are used as a springboard to further time together and ministry done in neighborhoods and more personal settings. Maybe the men and women each meet separately for breakfast or at another time weekly so they can dive into issues and personal struggles. Home groups often camp together or hold garage sales together. They picnic and worship together. They even go on mission trips together and feed the homeless in our own town as a group.

As people in groups honestly share, they begin to pray together and text encouraging verses to one another. In a medical situation, they go to the hospital together. They might pool money to meet a need. They help each other move if the need arises. They babysit so couples can have date nights. When a parenting issue comes up, wise counsel comes from someone in the group who has dealt with the issue before. The bottom line is that when stress hits (and it hits every believer), there is a "we are in this together" attitude.

In Matthew 13 Jesus tells of a farmer going out to sow seed for a future crop. As the farmer spread the seed by hand, some fell on the hard path where it could not penetrate the soil, and birds came and ate the seed. Some seed fell on rocky, shallow soil. Plants grew immediately, but the roots could not go deep. When the sun came out, the plants were scorched and died. Some seed fell on soil that could definitely grow plants, but thorns choked out the good seed and the plants intended by the sower died. Finally, some seed fell on good soil and there was a great harvest.

Jesus made the point that many people hear and respond to the gospel message, but over time many will not produce fruit and demonstrate true discipleship. The soils represent us. The seed represents the gospel, and it always has the power to grow something amazing. But each person has to decide if the seed will be allowed to grow. The seed has within it the power to produce fruit, yet as I read this parable, I believe the soil has responsibility to participate. Every person who receives the seed is potentially good soil that can produce much fruit. But every believer's soil also contains rocks and weeds that God will point out. I believe the gospel seed will find the weeds and the rocks in our lives, and this will leave us with a choice. He will give us the power to move the rocks and thorns, but we must choose. How do we move the obstacles? I believe we move them with God's strength (His Holy Spirit), with the directions given in His Word (the Bible), and with the help of His people (the church).

Let's put Galatians 6:2 into this picture. It instructs us to help carry one another's burdens. Some rocks and weeds are so big we cannot remove them from our lives alone. In fact, we were not meant to. God's plan was that we remove the obstacles together. Part of being filled with the Holy Spirit means we give to others the grace and help that God has already given to us and can give them through us. We don't judge or condemn people when a new rock or weed comes to light and needs to be removed. We aren't quick to offer advice or tell them a better way until we have heard them out and showed that we care. As we earn the right through relationship, the one in trouble allows us to help carry the burden.

All the while we allow them to speak into our lives as well. We work the field of our lives together. Empathy is the ability to take upon ourselves what someone else must be feeling. We put ourselves in their shoes. We don't just notice the rock; we begin to understand how it got there. We understand how the devil used lies to plant the rock or the weed, and why our friend has held on to that burden for so long. That rock feels like a protection or as though it's helping them escape from something, and the lies are strong. Together we are able to get rid of what one person alone could not hope to remove.

Recently I shared a personal struggle with a friend. After listening, he shared that he had a similar issue. This helped me realize I wasn't the only one who struggled. He prayed for me and allowed me to pray for him. He asked how he could help, and I told him just listening really made a difference and that he could ask me about it next time we met. He did better than that. He began to text me daily that he was praying for me. To encourage me, he sent me a daily Bible verse for more than a month.

It's a beautiful way of doing life, the way Jesus designed life to be lived.

The Power of a Community of Believers

James 5:14–15 asks, "Is anyone among you sick? Let them call the elders of the church to pray over them and anoint them with oil in the name of the Lord. And the prayer offered in faith will make the sick person well; the Lord will raise them up. If they have sinned, they will be forgiven."

It's important to note that this Greek word for sick is *astheneō*. It means to be weak or deficient in strength, to doubt, hesitate, be unsettled, or timid. It's a much more encompassing concept than physical sickness. The word can mean a person has a weak faith or a weak conscience. It can refer to a person who is weary or has grown morally or spiritually weak. This broader definition makes sense when we hear James's instruction to call the elders to anoint the person with oil and pray over them. Then we reach these great words in James 5:16: "Therefore confess your sins to each other and pray for each other so that you may be healed. The prayer of a righteous person is powerful and effective."

That's what true relationship looks like. I don't know about you, but there are times in my life when I sin and confess it to God, but the shame and guilt still plague me. God has certainly forgiven the sin, but fellowship with God still feels broken. When I confess my sin to trusted people, they minister to me and remind me that God is forgiving and separates me from my sin as far as the east is from the west. That's the power of togetherness at work. As mature Christians, we know God primarily speaks through His Word, yet sometimes His message comes best through other believers. A parallel passage, 1 Thessalonians 5:14, tells us to "encourage the disheartened" and "help the weak."

As I write this book, my wife and I are in the process of selling a house and buying another. If you've ever done that, you know how stressful and unsettling it can be. Added to that, there has been increased craziness at the church and I have not been sleeping well. The other evening my son Christian and his wife, Kiela, were hanging out with my wife and me. I grew tired and went to bed early.

A few minutes passed, then my son came into my bedroom and said, "Dad, can I talk to you for a minute? I am a little worried about you. I've been noticing that you and Mom are not getting along very well right now. You've been pretty irritable with her. Are you okay? Is all this pressure getting to you? There must be something going on, this isn't like you. Do you want to talk about it?"

My son and I have the type of relationship where we tell each other what's truly going on. I was able to confess that I had been overworking and not trusting Jesus enough. We talked for a while, and then he asked if he could pray for me. I said yes, and the prayer was healing and restorative. The next morning I got the opportunity to ask my wife for forgiveness.

Imagine that—my son wasn't calling me out, he was calling me up. Calling someone out can be judgmental and embarrasses them, but humbly reminding people who they are in Christ and coming alongside to help them calls them *up* to Christ.

This is exactly what James is talking about. My son didn't judge or condemn me. His intention was to help me and my wife; I had been stressed and hadn't even noticed that I'd been sharp with her. But the Bible says the "wounds from a friend can be trusted" (Prov. 27:6). Real spiritual maturity is us knowing and loving others and others knowing and loving us too.

Becoming Reconcilers

What prevents us from being known by others? Proverbs 18:1 paints a picture of a person holding himself at arm's length from others and the chaos that results. The NASB says, "He who *separates* himself seeks his own desire, he quarrels against all sound wisdom," and the ESV says, "Whoever *isolates* himself" (emphases added). The result is a fight against all that's good and wise and solid and true.

If we isolate ourselves, it's usually because we've been hurt. We've stuck our heart out and somebody trampled on it, so we vowed we'd never be vulnerable again. If this characterizes your life, I encourage you to find people you can trust. They are out there. Know this: If you don't believe they are out there, then you have accepted a lie from the enemy as truth.

When you pray for good friends, the Lord will bring those people into your life. Yes, the process seldom comes without hard work. It means making time to develop real relationships, taking a chance, and being honest about your fears and expectations. You will be disappointed at times because people fail. We must forgive one another and become adept at reconciliation. You will fail others too. You must encourage these new friends to be honest with you as well so you can ask for forgiveness and continue doing life together.

Jesus made it clear that God is love. As already established, God gives the love needed rather than what is deserved. From the fall in the Garden of Eden onward, we became God's enemies. But God sent Jesus to end the war for all who were ready to surrender. God is a peacemaker.

God calls us to be peacemakers too, and Jesus said blessed are the peacemakers. It means we simply reflect the priorities and character of God. Paul tells us we have been reconciled to God through Christ and given the ministry of reconciliation (2 Cor. 5:19). We now are empowered by the Holy Spirit to play a part in bringing peace to a war-torn world. "Reconciliation" means that broken or opposing things are put together again. Issues are settled. Understanding and harmony are achieved. Most importantly, God has given us the task of bringing peace to broken relationships.

This begins with helping people establish a relationship with God through Christ. Yet the reconciliation process continues as we become people who make peace with other people. Reconciliation starts in our own lives when we care more about others than we do about ourselves. This lifestyle alone will end many fights that result from selfishness in our own relational circles. When we see people struggling with relationships, we seek to put out the fires of frustration rather than stoke them. We are not enthralled by conflict like a kid on the playground running to see a good fight. Instead, we desire people to experience real relationship, so we seek to speak forgiveness and peace into every broken interaction.

Though it hurts when someone lets us down, it doesn't surprise us because we know every person is broken. We know there is miscommunication and confusion. We know our sinful nature is self-serving, and we know others struggle with the same thing. We are aware that the spiritual enemy of our souls works to divide us. The devil constantly seeks to slip seeds of discontent and division into the soil of our lives and relationships. While our heavenly Father is a reconciler, the devil is a divider. So when (not *if*) people hurt us or we hurt them, the enemy will whisper that we are better alone. Or the enemy will whisper that the grass is greener somewhere else. That the relationships we have are not worth fighting for, so we should find different ones, always searching for the perfect relationships—ones that are easy and don't take much work. He will try to water the seed of division that eventually grows into a bitter root.

The person who seeks to be alone often hurts others the most, because he repels people who need and want relationship with him. But if we allow the Holy Spirit and the Word of God and the people of God to help us restore what has been broken, we receive the benefit of living as we were created to live. In a world of broken people, the only hope of gaining what we were designed for is to become great forgivers and reconcilers. Where there is forgiveness we can help others, and we can be helped rather than struggling alone.

The whole point of the Ecclesiastes passage (supported by other passages) is to show us that life doesn't work when we isolate ourselves. Ecclesiastes shows a guy who's all alone. He's working his brains out. Why? To get more of what the world promises will satisfy. The passage reveals that he has work to do and the wealth that work produces, but what he doesn't have is anything that satisfies his soul. He hasn't spent his time, energy, and effort on what gives lasting peace, significance, and purpose.

This is the perfect picture of today's American culture. We love to work hard because in our mind our work gives us value, defines who we are, and can ultimately satisfy with what it provides. We strive to get ahead because life is a competition to see who can get the most. Life for many is about proving their worth to themselves and to the world. It's so sad that, for most, proving themselves leads to being alone. Why alone? Most often because the time it takes to prove themselves to the world is the time it would take to build relationship. We often want more because we have been promised more will fill the hole in our heart—but it doesn't. Again we end up discovering this to be true after we have lost that which we truly need—relationship. In the end, all this striving leaves us unsatisfied and weary, hurt, and disillusioned.

Stepping Out into New Relationships

When I write about "leadership," many think only of the pastor and official church leaders. It's true that the leadership of the church is needed and a part of God's plan for His church. But the Bible is also clear that all who are saved are disciples of Jesus and are supposed to learn how to help others become disciples. The leadership task of every believer, then, is to begin to get people together in relationship so we can help grow ourselves and others toward Christlikeness.

For some, the first step may be to accept that God made us for relationship with people. We must put our excuses aside and take a step of faith forward. We must risk stepping out into the relational waters because Jesus commanded us to.

For others with just Christian "acquaintances," our first step is to be more intentional in deepening friendships. With them, we must share our biblical perspective of relationships and invite them into something better.

For those who already lead small groups, it means moving beyond an "information only" Bible study, leading our group to live out the Scripture in a relational community where we really know and help one another. We start by sharing our expectations with the group.

In our church we use the summer to train our group leaders as well as give them a break. Rather than having a weekly group, we go camping and have barbecues and just hang out. As the summer comes to an end, we begin to re-form groups, which means we branch into new groups when we have a leader who is ready. As I write this, I am beginning a new home group tonight. My apprentice from last year is taking two families and adding two more. In my group, I have three couples from last year and three new families. Both groups will start out tonight sharing the vision for our journey together this year. They need to know what's expected, and be reminded often.

In my group I tell them we are going to study the Bible together. I'll also tell them they must be committed to becoming a spiritual family. I will expect them to be consistent in attendance and also to be in church on Sundays; a home group is not designed to replace the corporate gathering for worship and service. I'll tell them I'll call them if they miss a week, so they shouldn't be surprised. I call because I take the responsibility of a shepherd seriously. I want the group to become more than just a "destination" group, a place where we meet only once a week—I want us to do life together. I'll make sure that the group knows we are in a discipleship process. My goal as leader is to help everyone grow in Christ and become disciple-makers.

During the weekly home group times, I want everyone to join in the discussion. I know some in the group are shy, but over time I will press them a bit to share what they are thinking. I know some speak easily in front of others and some don't. So I will help everyone be involved, and I'll do so gently. I will ask them to minister to one another during the week by calling anyone who missed. I may ask a person to tell the Bible story or to make a meal for someone in the group who is sick. I involve an apprentice who will lead from time to time, and I'll be looking for others. I'll explain that what is said in the group stays in the group. I will explain what gossip is and how it can hurt relationship. I will let them know that if I feel the boundaries have been broken in this area, I will gently remind them, and I want them to do the same with me.

I'll share that one quality of a growing Christian is courage. When something happens between you and someone else that you do not understand or that bothers you, you must do what Scripture says and go lovingly and humbly to the person involved. Also, when someone shares in the group, there is no cross talk—everyone must listen while another person talks. There is no cutting people off; people must be allowed to say what they need to say. And there must be no immediate movement to fix others. Remember, we are trying to create a safe group where people can really begin to know and trust each other.

I'll tell them that when studying the Bible, we must look for how the Scriptures point us toward real relationship. All the Law and Prophets point to love for God and others, so every part of Scripture instructs us closer toward real relationship. As leaders, we begin to ask open-ended questions that point people toward practical ways everyone in the group can live out the teaching within community. For instance, Galatians 6:1–2 says,

> Brothers and sisters, if someone is caught in a sin, you who live by the Spirit should restore that person gently. But watch yourselves, or you also may be tempted. Carry each other's burdens, and in this way you will fulfill the law of Christ.

Notice what names Paul uses for people he is writing to: brothers and sisters. As we study, I'll ask a question like,

"What does he mean by calling them this?" Then, "What kind of brothers and sisters do you have in the physical world?" This gets group members to open up about their home lives.

As we go further, I ask them, "What does he mean by getting 'caught' in some kind of sin? Does he mean caught like a man cheating on his wife, or caught like a bird in a trap?" I will ask if they have ever known someone or been someone caught in a trap (some kind of sin trap). I will begin to share some of my story about how I have been caught in sin in my past. I will share about a person who helped me get free from that trap and how thankful I am. I might share about a person who hurt me by the way he dealt with me. I'll ask, "What would it look like to carry a burden someone has?" In this context there was a trapped person, and someone pointed out his condition gently and without pride, for his good. I might ask how we can help carry a burden in a situation like that. Bible teaching can be informational, but it also must lead toward openness, real relationship, and life transformation.

At the end of the session, we always ask for prayer requests. I try to set the tone by sharing a personal struggle. I ask for prayer and then invite someone else who would like to share. It's always quiet at first, but as time goes on, people begin. We also share victories, and often people have experienced God's blessing through another group member.

A Word of Caution

As a caveat, we must be careful about whom we choose to be in relationship with. Scripture is clear that bad company corrupts good morals. Jesus warned us about casting pearls before swine, and Paul warned us not to be unequally yoked with nonbelievers. We must be careful whom we give our heart to. Yes, we want to reach the lost and, yes, we want church people to grow into mature Christians. But the Bible clearly warns us that relationships are precious and can affect us in negative ways if we are not careful.

There are people we should be in relationship with and others we should be careful around. Some have no desire to follow Jesus and even wish to draw us away from the Lord, so we must keep at a safe distance. Some are not believers but are open to hear about Jesus, so we look for ways to bridge the gap. It takes wisdom to know how each kind of relationship should look. Others like the idea of relationship but sabotage it with their mouths, sometimes without even knowing it. When gossip has become part of their lives, it will take time to change, provided they even want to. This is why a discerning spiritual leader is needed to promote and protect a healthy environment. While no one is perfect, we must choose to be in transparent relationships only with those who want to be all that God wants. A person must be willing to obey Scripture. He or she must be willing to struggle and deal with conflict because real relationships aren't easy, yet those relationships must be two-way streets. Some people are not willing to do the hard work.

Don't pour out your whole heart at the beginning of a new relationship. Take time to make sure the people you are with are trustworthy (not perfect—that would mean you would always be alone). Give them some smaller things first, and then see what they do. If they make a mistake, don't just write them off. Address them in love and see how they respond.

You may find that they are broken in ways they don't even know. They may live the way they do because no loving, courageous brother or sister has ever confronted them in love, so they have a huge blind spot.

Part of creating a transparent relationship is being committed to others even when they fail you. The relational journey entails discovery. Every person has rules for relationship, and part of the journey is to discover theirs.

In my relationship with my wife, we have had several similar challenges to overcome through the years. I grew up in a home where we were taught that being late was a sign of disrespect toward others, so one of my relational rules is that people need to be on time. But one of my wife's relational rules is that it's okay to be "generally" on time. This has caused conflicts, and we've had to come up with a game plan that respected both perspectives.

The point is that as we begin to create authentic relationships where we help one another grow and thrive—it won't be without struggles. Many Christians run from anything that makes them uncomfortable, but this is the opposite of faith. Faith will lead us to continually step out into the unknown, uncomfortable by nature. We were chosen for just such a journey.

As you begin this journey, you will discover that God brings people into your life you can really connect with if you truly invest. But He will also bring people who don't appear to add much because they are so different or broken. I have often been surprised at how far I have been from the truth at first glance. Some of my closest friends were people who seemed to be nothing but relational vacuum cleaners at first. It's amazing how God can change things.

Hard Love

Sometimes we are faced with a chronically needy person who is always asking things from us but isn't in a place to give back. What happens then? A couple of things help sort this out.

First, we must help others not because they deserve our help but because Christ commands us to and because we love and want to follow Him. A willingness to do so—even if we don't have the desire to do so—tells us that the Holy Spirit is working in our hearts. Maybe a person doesn't deserve our help, but that does not mean we won't help them. We need to ask ourselves, did we deserve help when Jesus came for us?

Second, we must continually ask ourselves what is the most loving thing we can do for a person. Sometimes the best help we can give (particularly if this person has shown a habit of not being dependable or kind) is to not bail them out of a hard spot. If we always rush to help this person, then we might be enabling them to keep going in a harmful direction. Much discernment is needed in these situations.

As I already mentioned, my son Christian, a drug addict at the time, once lived in a homeless shelter because he had exhausted all other options. I had given much help to him already, but he continually made poor choices, so I knew the most loving thing I could do for him was to allow him to sit in this homeless shelter for a while. It wasn't an easy decision, and others disagreed with me. But my intention wasn't to judge him or make his life more difficult. It was to love him enough to leave him in a hard spot, because that's what he needed at that moment. He needed to reach rock bottom if he was ever going to move forward and up.

If an alcoholic is crying out for a drink, you don't help him by giving him another drink. Every day my son was in the shelter was another day of living pain for my wife and me, probably more painful for us than for him. But we knew if we were to love him best, we would have to suffer the pain of separation and fear. We knew he needed to be there, and it was there that God did His best work.

What does it mean to truly help others? True love and fellowship and friendship must also be wise. We must help people in the truth of God's Word. We must continually ask ourselves the famous question, "What would Jesus do?" while also asking another trickier, more nuanced question, "What would Jesus *have me* do?"

When we help others, we must abide in Christ ourselves if we are to have the wisdom and strength needed—especially when people are difficult. We must continually invest time in our relationship with Jesus if we are to create a culture that is more than "just us and Jesus." It sounds counterintuitive, but it's not. If oxygen masks come down in the cabin of a plane, parents must put on their own masks before helping their children put on theirs. As we abide in Christ (the vertical portion of abiding), we are reminded that we are imperfect and God saved us. This humbles us as we also remember that He continues to pour out His grace to us. As we spend time with Jesus, we start to care about what He cares about, and this motivates us to reach out to and spend time with others (the horizontal part of abiding).

If we abide in Christ, then we will see things the way Christ sees them. The point is, when people tell us their troubles, our response is, "Yep, I've got problems too, and I know my Redeemer lives. That's why we can go to Jesus together.

Because we all need grace." We are helpers, not accusers. We are fellow heirs (Rom. 8:17).

If our walk with Christ is suffering, then it's much harder to truly help people. When I am not close to Christ, I care very little for others. When I am distant from Jesus, I don't have the discernment to know there is something amiss. I can easily misdiagnose a problem and end up relying on my experience rather than the Holy Spirit to guide me. It's like a drowning man trying to help a drowning man—little good comes from it. When we spend time with Jesus, we recognize our brokenness, and this forces us to deal with the log in our own eye. We become helpers of others rather than accusers. Then we can see clearly enough to help our hurting friends as grace flows to us and through us.

The Warmth of a Fire

The passage from Ecclesiastes also hints at intimacy. Not sexual intimacy necessarily, except in husband and wife relationships, but the type of close relationship between friends where real honesty exists.

Let's look back at our passage in Ecclesiastes: "If two lie down together, they will keep warm. But how can one keep warm alone?" (4:11). When the night gets cold, body heat sustains us like a burning bundle of twigs and branches. We North Idahoans well know that you need more than one log to build a fire. Once the fire's lit, if you take a log away from that fire and isolate it, its flame will die. But if you keep the log with the others, then the fire will stay stoked and provide heat for a long time.

The same is true for our spiritual lives. If a person becomes isolated, there is little warmth to keep the spiritual fire burning. But when a person is surrounded by other believers who are also on fire, then there is spiritual sustenance for the long haul.

First John 1:5–7 talks about the deep fellowship we can have with other believers.

> This is the message we have heard from him and declare to you: God is light; in him there is no darkness at all. If we claim to have fellowship with him and yet walk in the darkness, we lie and do not live out the truth. But if we walk in the light, as he is in the light, we have fellowship with one another, and the blood of Jesus, his Son, purifies us from all sin.

If we abide in Christ, if we walk in the light, then Jesus is our power source to bear fruit. When we abide in Christ, it doesn't simply mean we fellowship with Jesus only. It means that we fellowship both with Jesus and with other believers, and we find intimacy, sustenance, strength, ability to weather storms, and strength to do the tasks God gives us. We go through both good times and troubled times together.

The question is, do you have these kinds of relationships? If not, then you are trying to live on a faith that is other than God designed. You won't have the strength you will need because the recipe is missing an important ingredient.

9

Defeating the Enemy Together

I mentioned that I wrestled competitively in high school and college, and I learned a certain way of approaching life from participating in that sport. Over the years the sport developed in me a kind of warrior mind-set. Physical and mental aggressiveness and perseverance are part of the mentality. To win, you must battle with those who make combat a way of life. The training is extreme and the discipline it takes borders on craziness. Thinking back, I wonder what in the world gets into people to make them willing to do what we did to our bodies.

Not only do you face an opponent, but an internal battle goes on all the time. You have to watch others eating and abstain. You have to watch others relax while you run and lift and practice, often twice a day. You watch others being cheered on in the sport they play (like basketball or football) while few sit in the stands cheering you on. At a practice or a match, those who don't understand the sport think it's just a battle of strength, but it's far from it. Strategy plays a much larger part. You must be able to win the mental game and do it when completely exhausted. To become great at wrestling, it has to become a lifestyle—you can't "kind of" do it and still win.

Although today I no longer competitively wrestle, I apply many of the principles of the sport to being a Christian, discipling others, and walking in faith as the body of Christ. Some Christians have been told that Jesus promises the battle is over once you become a Christian, but that is far from the truth. As I have written before, Scripture reveals that when we are born again we are born into a war. We do not live in peacetime. We live in an ongoing battle for the souls of men. The Bible has many passages that describe this fight—how we need to train for battle, how we must wrestle and contend for the truth, how we do not need to fear this fight because God fights for and with us, how the battle belongs to the Lord, and how we are ultimately blessed when we persevere and in the end triumph for the sake of Jesus.

As a wrestler I understood this kind of biblical language and imagery pretty quickly. But I also got that it was not a battle I could fight alone. That may surprise you because you think of wrestling as an individual sport, but it's not really. A wrestler absolutely needs a coach. He needs mentors who show him the moves and guide him along. He needs fellow wrestlers—partners—for training and development. A wrestler must practice a move a thousand times with someone who lets him do the move with little resistance before he can do a move on someone with full resistance and succeed. We call this drilling, and practice means doing the move over and over again at an increasingly faster pace as you grow in the sport. Not only is this exhausting, but it develops muscle memory that will lead to success in a real match.

Growing as a partner is vital in wrestling, because without a good partner, you cannot become a great wrestler. Coaching is also so important because when you go full speed, you cannot see the mistakes you are making, so you need someone outside watching to help you improve. You also need support emotionally and physically. When you are in a combat sport, there comes a time when you must go out on the mat (or in the cage or the ring) alone to face your opponent. However, long before you step out there, you have been surrounded by a team that helped you to get ready. Long after you come off the mat, you have a team that helps you deal with what happened, both good and bad. Your trainers help ease the pain from the bruises and strains and prepare you for your next match.

But it's still easy to feel down, because no one succeeds all the time. You will fail so often that you'll wonder if you should just give it up. It's then that support and encouragement make such a big difference. Sometimes you're so tired that you don't think you can go on, but your coaches and teammates push you forward and encourage you to go beyond what you thought you could. Seeing others push through their pain helps you keep going through your own. The celebration with others when you win makes the win so much more meaningful. When people are waiting to embrace you after the fight is over, it really is meaningful and fulfilling. The common experience binds us together at the heart level. You see, wrestling is really a team sport.

The same is true of our spiritual lives. Many Christians fail when "fight night" comes because they haven't had the team every day. A time comes when they must stand against injustice with grace and truth, and they say nothing or they immaturely say something that isn't Christlike. A chance to witness comes, and they don't know what to say. A decision must be made to get off the internet when they are alone, and they don't. A marriage gets tough, and they should remain committed, but they don't.

Most Christians have not experienced team in their spiritual walk. They have falsely believed that Christianity is an individual sport, so to speak. Oh, they do many things with lots of people. But when no one knows what's going on in their real life, and they don't know what to do with what's filling them with confusion or doubt, then they are still truly alone. The truth is, when we don't share the successes, they mean less. When we don't share the hurts, they hurt more. When we don't train spiritually with a good partner and coach, we don't get better. We tend to just keep making the same mistakes over and over again. Oftentimes this leads to not finishing the race we started.

You see, all our spiritual battles, even our individual battles, can—and should—be fought in relationship with other believers. We are in this fight together. Our brothers and sisters in Christ are our fellow teammates. We stand shoulder to shoulder with other sons and daughters of our Father, and Christ calls us to victory as a body, not just as individuals.

That's my question for you. Do you know you're not alone in this fight?

The Battle Exists. Period.

If you travel to Israel today, you'll notice a curious thing to American eyes. Everywhere you look there are soldiers, and they are all armed. In the United States you might see a soldier now and then, or maybe a convoy of military vehicles out on the freeway, or a news piece about soldiers. But in Israel, soldiers are everywhere. You go get a cup of coffee, and soldiers are at the coffee shop. You get on a bus, and soldiers are on the bus. You see schoolchildren out on a field trip, and each group of students has an armed soldier protecting them.

Soldiers are everywhere in Israel for at least two reasons. First, because Israel is a country that constantly sees warfare—it is surrounded by enemies. Some of Israel's neighbors have pledged to "push Israel into the sea." As a result, Israel is always on the alert. Second, because military service is compulsory in Israel—for both men and women. Every person in Israel must be in the military from ages eighteen to twenty. As a result, basically the whole population is either going to be a soldier, is a soldier now, or has been a soldier and is familiar with fighting strategy. After you do your two years, you become a member of the reserves until age fifty-five. Every year you spend a month training with the reserves so you are ready if and when the next attack comes. Many in Israel keep their military pack and weapons by their door just in case the alarm is sounded. They have every reason to consider themselves citizen soldiers, in a state of readiness, perpetually at war. In their daily lives, they never forget that they do not live in a world at peace.

That's the kind of existence we're called to as Christians. Constant vigilance. Constant battle. Constant participation in the army. Just like all modern Israelis see themselves as soldiers, so must all Christians see themselves as in a war. The battles we wage as Christians are not physical battles as in Israel. They're spiritual battles, "not against flesh and blood, but against the rulers, against the authorities, against the powers of this dark world and against the spiritual forces of evil in the heavenly realms" (Eph. 6:12).

The good news is, we don't need to fight the battles all alone—in fact, we are not supposed to. Let's go back again to Ecclesiastes 4:12: "Though one may be overpowered, two can defend themselves. A cord of three strands is not quickly broken." The writer closes this passage by noting there's a battle going on. The battle exists. Period. One person fighting alone can be overpowered. But if two people fight side by side, on the same team, then they can win together. Even better than two, are three.

Citizen Soldiers

As I have written, in the world we live in presently, we don't live in peacetime; we live in a war zone. But many Christians forget that. It's easy to do this when there are so-called spiritual leaders seeking to convince them that with enough faith their problems and roadblocks to personal comfort will go away. It's easy to grow complacent in a world drawing us into the false belief that comfort is our highest aim and this world is the best and only thing there is. We mistakenly think the Christian life is all about having problem-free families, or enough money to own two new cars and live in a nice house in the suburbs, or living "our best life now."

Yes, Jesus gives us a sense of internal peace in spite of the war we live in (John 14:27), but nowhere in Scripture does the Lord promise us problem-free lives. To the contrary, the Bible often points to the unavoidable reality of tribulation, trials, and persecution. We know as Christians it's not *if* there's a battle. It's already happening. *We have a battle. The battle is on our hands right now.* The moment we become saved is the moment we become aware of the source of the struggle and that we are soldiers.

The reality of constant spiritual warfare is crucial for believers to understand. Too often Christians become disappointed when things don't go our way. The problem is that we have unmet expectations. We become Christians and then falsely believe battles are over. If we believe our lives should be problem-free, and a fight comes along, then we think there's something wrong. Maybe we've fallen out of God's favor, we wonder. Why doesn't God simply take this battle away and give us whatever we want? This is why true discipleship is so important. A new believer needs to know how we got to this time in history. How did things get this way? What does God want us to do in our slice of history? What should we expect? How ought we to live? All these questions need to be answered by the spiritual coaches and teammates God has positioned in His church. This is why evangelism without discipleship is not biblical and even dangerous.

So many Christians see any kind of struggle and discomfort as something to be avoided rather than a call to fight. Sadly, this affects what a church can do in a broken world. The devil needs only to bring our expectations to nothing to cause believers to doubt the message they heard.

The devil has a different method for dealing with unbelievers, however. He needs to only "manage" them as they travel a worldly course toward destruction. He doesn't care which worldly path they take, as long as they don't take the narrow road to salvation. He doesn't mind if they find the world's version of happiness because it keeps them distracted. However, his lies eventually lead to death, because death is a part of the fallen world, and the devil by his very nature is a murderer and a thief (John 10:10).

Unbelievers are already being swept downstream with the cultural current that the devil has manipulated to take them away from real value and eternal life. The believer must fight upstream and seek to hold fast rather than relax and allow the current to take him. The devil's energy is used in battles against those who seek to thwart him and take away those he has captured.

The Bible is clear that believers actually wage war on two fronts. The first battle happens in our minds, and it's the battle for righteous thinking. There is a conflict going on within us as believers. God's Word tells us that we were once controlled by our sinful nature, our appetites, but now the Holy Spirit has entered our hearts when we received what Jesus has done for us. The decision we must make is either to set our minds on what the flesh desires or to live in accordance with the Spirit and set our minds on what the Spirit desires (Rom. 8:6–8). We must not allow ourselves to be conformed to the pattern of this world, but to be transformed by the renewing of our minds (Rom. 12:2). This transformation happens as we take captive every thought and make it obedient to Christ. Second Corinthians 10:3–5 tells us that the weapons we use are not the weapons of the world, but they have power to destroy every argument that sets itself up against the knowledge of God. The conflict goes on daily as we seek to deny ourselves and take up our cross and follow Jesus. Paul wrote in Philippians that many will make their appetites their god and it will lead to the destruction of their souls as well as their relationships. This first battle can be won only as we hold on to the Word with the help of the Holy Spirit and other fellow spiritual wrestling team members.

The second battle relates to the first but is slightly different. This is the overall battle against the devil. It's the battle *against* everything the devil espouses, and the battle *for* everything God espouses. First Peter 5:8 says, "Be alert and of sober mind. Your enemy the devil prowls around like a roaring lion looking for someone to devour." As Christians, we are soldiers of light. The world has been captured by the enemy, yet Paul invites, "Join with me in suffering, like a good soldier of Christ Jesus" (2 Tim. 2:3).

The good news is that the battles have ultimately already been fought and won by Christ on the cross. Hebrews 2:14–15 says, "Since the children have flesh and blood, [Jesus] too shared in their humanity so that by his death he might break the power of him who holds the power of death—that is, the devil—and free those who all their lives were held in slavery by their fear of death." Jesus is victorious, and as Christians, we are victorious also with the help of the Word of God, the Spirit of God, and the people of God. We never should ignore these battles, but we do not need to be afraid of these battles either. When it comes to spiritual warfare, one of my favorite verses is 1 John 4:4, which says, "The one who is in you [Jesus] is greater than the one who is in the world [the devil]."

Although Jesus is greater than Satan, our spiritual battles continue because the devil is still alive and at work on planet Earth. First John 5:19 says, "We know that we are children of God, and that the whole world is under the control of the evil one." This verse is not saying Satan is in charge of the whole world and its future. To the contrary, God is always ultimately in charge. God in His sovereignty always has been and always will be in control of the outcome. As Psalm 33:11 says, "The LORD's plans stand firm forever; his intentions can never be shaken" (NLT).

But 1 John 5:19 says that the whole world lies in the power of the evil one. Though Satan is a defeated enemy and his serpent head has ultimately been crushed, he still has fangs full of venom (Gen. 3:15). Satan's entire mission is to steal and kill and destroy (John 10:10), and we can see evidences of this vicious work in the hearts and lives of people everywhere today. Many people love the darkness and their deeds are evil (John 3:19).

Romans 6:23 says the "wages of sin is death." Satan constantly seeks to lull Christians to sleep by using the culture to exhaust us as we use our available energy to get what it offers. You see, Satan has designed a culture around enticing the sinful nature he knows is within every human heart. He takes advantage of our weakness by creating offers that promise a solution that will feed the brokenness in us. He also does his best to get us to forget there is a puppet master pulling the strings of the manipulative culture. His desire for believers is that we get caught up in the culture to the extent that we do not play the part He has given us to play in the rescue mission to save the lost. When we forget the reality of the enemy, it's then that an ambush works best. When people forget a lion exists, it makes a perfect environment for him to pounce.

Are we in a battle? Absolutely. Christians cannot coast in the faith because the cultural river is created to drag us downstream. All we need do to find ourselves miles from where God intended is to just relax. We can't simply become followers of Jesus and then expect no challenges. But the good news is that we don't need to battle spiritually alone. The victory is ours in Jesus.

The Spiritual Forces in the Heavenly Realms

What's the solution to winning spiritual battles? The Ecclesiastes passage points to strength in numbers. A person fighting by himself can be overpowered, but if that one gets another to help him (or maybe two, or three, or four, or five), then he's going to survive and be victorious. That's the church—the power of the body of Christ, all fighting on the same side together.

Ephesians 6:10–20 is perhaps the best known passage about what to do in a battle.

> Finally, be strong in the Lord and in his mighty power. Put on the full armor of God, so that you can take your stand against the devil's schemes. For our struggle is not against flesh and blood, but against the rulers, against the authorities, against the powers of this dark world and against the spiritual forces of evil in the heavenly realms. Therefore put on the full armor of God, so that when the day of evil comes, you may be able to stand your ground, and after you have done everything, to stand. Stand firm then, with the belt of truth buckled around your waist, with the breastplate of righteousness in place, and with your feet fitted with the readiness that comes from the gospel of peace. In addition to all this, take up the shield of faith, with which you can extinguish all the flaming arrows of the evil one. Take the helmet of salvation and the sword of the Spirit, which is the word of God.

And pray in the Spirit on all occasions with all kinds of prayers and requests. With this in mind, be alert and always keep on praying for all the Lord's people. Pray also for me, that whenever I speak, words may be given me so that I will fearlessly make known the mystery of the gospel, for which I am an ambassador in chains. Pray that I may declare it fearlessly, as I should.

This contains so many good directives for us. But as I related earlier, the overall context of Ephesians 6 (and the whole book of Ephesians, for that matter) is that it's written to the whole church. Note the opening salutation in Ephesians 1:1–2: "Paul, an apostle of Christ Jesus by the will of God, to God's holy people in Ephesus, the faithful in Christ Jesus: Grace and peace to you from God our Father and the Lord Jesus Christ."

That's us. We are the faithful in Christ Jesus. We are the family of God. We are the household of God. We are the body of Christ. When we understand the context of Ephesians 6, it means we put on personal armor for sure. But this is key: The Roman armor Paul is referring to could not be put on without the help of fellow soldiers. Some of the armor required others to place and secure it. (Some was tied in the back, so the soldier could not tie it himself.) Once the armor was on each individual, the soldiers were then called upon to fight together. The Romans succeeded in the world at their time because of their strategy and teamwork. Paul knew what he was doing when he referred to these mighty human warriors. Just as they did, we need to stand back-to-back and shoulder-to-shoulder because we are a spiritual army. Paul writes to a plurality of soldiers. If we fight the battle alone, then there's a good chance we'll be defeated. But together, fighting a spiritual enemy, we can triumph. As I wrote earlier, many like to use 1 Corinthians 13 as a marriage text even though it was written to the church. Christians also like to use Ephesians 6 as an individual battle plan rather than a church battle plan for spiritual warfare.

What does that mean for us as a body of believers? It points to the power of togetherness. As a church, we need to corporately stand firm in the Lord. As a church, we need to be strong in God's Word, truth, and righteousness. As a church, we need to be ready with the gospel of peace. As a church, we need to shield ourselves and each other with the shield of faith. As a church, we need to rely upon our salvation, prayer, and the Word of God.

Similarly, Peter encourages us, "Resist [the devil], standing firm in the faith, because you know that the family of believers throughout the world is undergoing the same kind of sufferings" (1 Pet. 5:9). That's a call for the whole family of God to resist the devil together. The joy and strength we get from relationships help us resist the devil.

I love the book of Nehemiah. The story is that some Hebrews who had been captured and sent to Babylon under King Nebuchadnezzar were allowed to return to Judah under King Artaxerxes to rebuild the wall around Jerusalem. Although the Israelites had the new king's blessing, it still proved a difficult task. The work was immense and arduous. There was much to do and workers were few and spread thinly along the breadth of the long circular wall. Then opposition rose and continued through most of the rebuilding process.

Nehemiah, who led the rebuilding, posted guards day and night to meet the threat. He encouraged the people not to be afraid, then finally turned every worker into a soldier. He wrote,

> Half of my men did the work, while the other half were equipped with spears, shields, bows and armor. The officers posted themselves behind all the people of Judah who were building the wall. Those who carried materials did their work with one hand and held a weapon in the other, and each of the builders wore his sword at his side as he worked. But the man who sounded the trumpet stayed with me.
>
> Then I said to the nobles, the officials and the rest of the people, "The work is extensive and spread out, and we are widely separated from each other along the wall. Wherever you hear the sound of the trumpet, join us there. Our God will fight for us!" (Neh. 4:16–20)

Let those images resound in your mind and heart. First, each worker had a tool in one hand and a sword in the other. The lesson? While you're working, always keep your weapons with you. Remain vigilant in ministry. Keep watchful and attentive in your spiritual walk. That's our call as Christians too. Paul reminds us in 1 Corinthians 16:13–14, "Be on your guard; stand firm in the faith; be courageous; be strong. Do everything in love."

And second, if the enemy comes to attack, we are to blow the trumpet, and everybody else will come to the aid of the one being attacked. We'll rally around the person who needs help the most. The lesson? We use our gifts and abilities to fight for each other, and we allow others to fight for us too. Each person, in this sense, is doing the work to protect the overall work of God as well as the personal part of the wall near their own house. We are each given the mandate to let the one with the trumpet know we are under attack so the troops can help us. We also are listening for the sound of the trumpet in case the enemy attacks someone else. We're supposed to make sure the trumpet is blown to signal a need. How will anybody know to rally around us unless we blow our trumpet and make our needs known?

This is so important for those who struggle with pride. You see, someone with pride may decide that they will go help if others need it, but they don't want to be the one who, in their own mind, ever is weak enough to need advice or support. As I discussed earlier, a spiritually mature person not only gives support but receives it as well. When the book of Nehemiah was written, the enemy was seeking to find a weak place in the wall so they could take the whole city from within. When someone fails to blow the trumpet though they are under attack, it affects everyone in the city because the enemy doesn't just want them; he wants to use that breach to take the whole place.

Pride can affect everyone in your physical and spiritual family, and it gives the devil an easy win. When we make decisions that affect us, it rarely affects only us. How many people were killed when David unwisely decided to take a census of the people even though he was warned not to by his wise counsel? How many people did Hezekiah's pride affect when he showed the Babylonian ambassadors all the treasure he had? How many died when Achan hid treasure under his tent? How many are affected in a church when a senior pastor or a volunteer leader chooses to sin or gives up because he is exhausted from doing the work alone? How many kids and spouses are affected when a dad or mom is under stress but doesn't ask for help or has no spiritual teammate to ask for help?

Toothless Lions and Isolated Gazelles

What might it look like to battle as a team? Last night I called about ten families in our church. This is something I do fairly regularly.

One man hadn't been to church in several weeks, and for quite a while prior to that he had not been nearly as faithful as he once had been. I wondered if everything was okay. It turned out he had lost his full-time job, so he was now working two part-time jobs. One was here and one was in Seattle, so he was traveling back and forth between the two every weekend. Along with this, he shared, his daughter needed surgery because of a serious health issue. Needless to say he was stressed. But nobody knew about his problems until I called. He was struggling in his faith because he was praying for a new job, but that prayer wasn't being answered. His marriage was hurting and he was worried about his child. The devil was attacking this man, shooting arrows at him, and his faith was growing weak. The man used to be a home group leader, but he had needed to step back because of time constraints. He wasn't in relationship with many people anymore or involved with the church. So he definitely needed help.

What's the solution? Part of the responsibility definitely lies with this man. He's the kind of man who would usually help someone else but was reluctant to let anyone help him. He needs to blow his trumpet and announce an attack. Others could rally to his side and fight for him. We could encourage him together, pray for him, be involved in his life, help him find another full-time job. We could help him with the shield of faith. But you see, part of the responsibility also lies within the body. If we are in relationship, we notice when someone is missing. We create a culture where we not only notice but step out to check on people when they stray or hide or hurt.

Another person I called was having problems in his marriage. He and his wife have both been Christians for years, but before they became Christians they were both sexually active. One of his wife's ex-boyfriends had reemerged, and this was causing flashes of anger in the husband's life. Fortunately, this man and his wife are both actively involved in a small group. They are doing life alongside people who aren't going to judge them. They can be in a safe environment to process this difficulty out loud. They can take their secrets out of darkness and put on the armor of light. The pressure gets released. People can pray for them and encourage them through their struggle.

This isn't always the case. So many people are not noticed when they begin to fade away, and they certainly don't think they should blow the trumpet when something is wrong (or at least not until things are so bad that it's hard to repair the damage). So often by the time a person comes to a pastor for help with a sin issue, the problem is extreme. The person has been caught doing porn or talking to an ex-boyfriend on Facebook. Maybe a full-on affair has begun and the marriage is in big trouble.

It's so sad that often people have no one who really knows them and could get involved long before the consequences become extreme. In the same way, I often see Christians who have tried to take on the temptations and spiritual attacks alone. They may become convinced that their sin is justified because they have it really rough, or they may believe their

struggles are not normal so no one could possibly understand. This kind of thinking can lead to guilt that so weighs
someone down that they believe God has abandoned them.
The pressure leads to giving in to sin and damage is done
to all involved.

The devil has quite a gig going on. He loves to tempt you,
and if you give in, he loves to convince you there is no way
you can be forgiven. Or he tells you a particular sin is not a
big deal and everyone is doing it, so go ahead. Besides, he tells
you that because you are covered by grace, you can just say
you are sorry later. Or if God didn't want you to go ahead,
He wouldn't have made this such a temptation or allowed
the opportunity to arise. You prayed about it and God didn't
take it away, so He must not mind—besides He doesn't want
you to be miserable—He wants you happy.

All these subtle messages are designed to lead you away
from the light into the darkness where the devil loves to play
in secret. But he's even smarter than that. He loves to tempt
you, and when you fight him off, he loves to tell you, "Yeah,
but you were tempted, so you are still evil." He loves to tell
you thinking it is just as bad as doing it, so you might as well
give in. Or if you were really a follower of Jesus, it would not
even be a temptation. By these devices, he gets to so many
of us, and the result is we don't feel we can or need to come
to the Father for forgiveness. Over time, we begin to become
either weighed down by guilt or immune to the Holy Spirit's
prompting to return—we may actually believe we can't.

But God gives us a better way. In the last chapter we unpacked James 5:16. Remember, we are called to confess our
sins one to another, and this can produce spiritual healing.
But this verse applies to this topic as well. The devil loves to

confuse us and lie to us. When we bring our sin struggles into the light of God's Word and the light of authentic relationship, the devil loses his hold on us. The devil is the master of darkness and loves to play in secret where he can distort, deceive, and kill. When we come out of the devil's fog and openly, regularly share our sin struggles with one another, we are reminded that we are not alone—others struggle too. First Corinthians 10:13 says, "No temptation has overtaken [us] except what is common to mankind."

As we relate to one another, we are able to share past failings so we can warn one another not to go down those roads. The devil tells us the consequences won't be huge, but in the light people share how their sin hurt themselves and others, and it's the devil's lie that sin won't have much impact.

If we are always living in the light of spiritual relationship with Jesus and others, then the lies don't get nearly as far, and the stronghold the devil would like to build in our lives isn't as large and deadly. When the devil whispers the lie that it's too late to return to the Lord, we can speak the truth to one another—God is always waiting for the prodigal to come home. When the devil convinces us that God doesn't care and we are in life alone, we can speak the truth that Jesus never leaves us. If we can help each other while the sin is just an idea, then it does not grow into a huge issue with horrible consequences.

The other day I was reading in 1 Peter where Peter writes about the devil prowling around like a roaring lion. It reminded me of a National Geographic special I'd seen years ago that showed how older male lions work together with healthy young lions to feed the whole pride. The old lions have lost their ability to do much—they have few teeth left and not much endurance, but they still play an important role. They still have their roar. The lions spot a herd of gazelles, and the younger lions set up, hiding in the grass around the edge of the herd. The old lions circle around and walk and roar, pushing the gazelles toward the hiding lions. Their intent is to scare the potential prey so they panic, divide, and run into the hiding lions. Often in their panic they run straight toward the younger lions. The irony is that the safest place to stay is together and unafraid of the roaring lion because he's the weakest of the threats. It's the same for us as believers. In our panic we end up running into problems rather than facing the loudest but weakest enemy.

There's a great lesson for us Christians. The devil has been defeated by Christ, yet the devil can still roar. The devil loves to separate us from the safety of other believers. When we're outside the herd, we're much more vulnerable. We tend to panic. We run every which way, sometimes into the open mouths of teeth-filled spiritual predators. When we're isolated, we're open to attack.

Here's a fact: No soldier wants to take on an opposing army all by himself. But when a soldier stands together with his outfit and fights, he stands tall with everybody who can help him in the cause. An entire army has infinitely more strength than an isolated soldier left alone.

Are you an isolated gazelle?

Are you a soldier trying to fight a war all by yourself?

We must make relationships a priority. If we're not in relationship with others, we will be forced to fight spiritual battles alone. We're not in a good place then. We're in danger. If we're isolated from other believers, the devil will distract us at first. He'll entice us with temptations that look good from the outside. He'll get us out of balance. And before long we're on a pathway to sin and death.

We were all built to be part of a family, a body, an army.

How Do People Make It?

Last year a single mother began to come to our home group. Her young husband had committed suicide and her young family was devastated. Our home group began to make them meals and go to her house to move his stuff out of sight. We helped her find a place to stay because she didn't want to be in the house, at least for a while. We later brought her groceries and cut her firewood so she had heat and did some other jobs around the house.

The people in our group were so amazing, and she quickly found she had friends who would carry her through her toughest time. The other women in the group started meeting with her to talk her through the situation, and she eventually gave her life to Jesus and so did her thirteen-year-old daughter.

This last week the mom started back to school so she can develop a career that will help her support her family. She had to take some core college classes, and immediately her newfound Christian faith came under attack. Her ethics teacher shared his disdain for Christianity and planted seeds in her mind that she didn't know what to do with. The devil was on the prowl and using the college as his playground. She came to group with several questions that had bothered her, and it was so amazing to watch her spiritual family surround her.

As we began to unpack the doubts the devil had planted, she saw there were easy answers to her questions that had sounded so profound and complex. She began to get so excited that she wanted to record everything everyone was saying and play it for the whole college class. We talked about how the devil works and the lies he tells.

As the night went on, one person (who just came to the Lord last year) said, "I wonder how people do the Christian life without a spiritual family? How do they make it when the devil tries to use our media and colleges to destroy our faith, and they don't have anyone to work through this stuff with?"

Unfortunately, too many Christians don't have a spiritual family and don't stand up under the pressure. God has given us everything we need for life and godliness (2 Pet. 1:3). But so many people are not using the tools He has provided, and not using the perfect spiritual recipe could fail to create a spiritual meal that will sustain them. Remember, that missing ingredient is relationship.

10

A City on a Hill

Too often Christians aren't taught that, as disciples of Jesus, they need to become spiritually mature disciple-makers. Even if they are taught that they need to mature, they don't know this is supposed to happen in a spiritual family. In biblical language, this means they were born again through faith in Christ so they moved from being spiritually dead to becoming a spiritual infant. Yet they remain spiritual infants because they are not fed spiritual food by their spiritual family. Sadly, this is the norm rather than the exception. Most of those who do end up becoming mature do so almost accidently as they go on a long journey that could have been far less painful for them and much more intentional and reproducible in the lives of others.

As a result of a lack of spiritual family and discipleship, most believers do not know they were God's plan A to make disciples, and they abdicate the responsibility to pastors.

Unfortunately most pastors have only learned to teach (transfer information nonrelationally) their way to more disciples. And so here we are—a mess that is clearly not working to represent Jesus well on planet Earth. How sad when a church is full of potential spiritual soldiers who could be released on a community but instead are relegated to spiritual infanthood— at best, theory-laden and needy spectators.

Some church leaders have countered this mistake by rightly teaching that every Christian can and should be a personal evangelist. They teach Christians how to live in such a way that, through relationship, they earn the right to share the gospel and help people join the family of God. In these churches, people are often trained in "personal evangelism" classes, and the idea behind these classes is spot-on. Christians are and should be taught that conversations about Jesus, the cross, repentance, forgiveness, and salvation happen best within the natural course of relationships. People are led to Jesus by individuals, not so much by a big event.

Don't get me wrong. I am not saying there is no purpose for events. Pastors who help people see their need for Christ and teach personal evangelism can also teach people to come together corporately to reach a community. This should be a both-and scenario. The fuller truth is that there are some things we can do together that we cannot pull off alone. We need to take advantage of every opportunity to reach lost people using our corporate resources. But there are some things that cannot happen best in an event. Wisdom is to know the difference.

In both situations, real relationship building is important. Not only do we earn the right to share our faith through relationship, but this same relationship enables us to walk through the stages of maturity with new believers. At our church, we often say we are "a hospital for the sick." But we are also like birthing rooms at the maternity ward where spiritual babies are being born because of relationship.

If you help birth a new believer, then you get to help raise them. This is such an important concept, because the church today is often simply a destination, a place to go. Instead, the church must be a place to build relationships, grow disciples, and serve.

Both the corporate and the relational pieces need to be included in a healthy church body. We are all called to join together into an organized and relational community that seeks to fulfill the mission. Jesus makes this clear when He tells us we are both a light that cannot be hidden and a city on a hill.

A Light and a City

Question: What is demonstrated when individuals are in relationship with one another as a church? Jesus introduces the concept of corporate evangelism in an exhortation to His disciples in Matthew 5:14–16:

> You are the light of the world. A town built on a hill cannot be hidden. Neither do people light a lamp and put it under a bowl. Instead they put it on its stand, and it gives light to everyone in the house. In the same way, let your light shine before others, that they may see your good deeds and glorify your Father in heaven.

Notice how Jesus begins with the concept, "light of the world." He's speaking to all His disciples here, us included, not just individuals within His immediate hearing. What does it mean to be the light of the world? In our modern culture, a light only works if it is plugged into a power source. The believer's power source is the Holy Spirit given at conversion. Jesus made it clear that we cannot be who we are called to be unless we abide in Him.

Jesus further reveals that light is given for a purpose—it shines on darkened places so people can walk safely. The light's job is to reveal anything that's hiding that can potentially hurt us. Light represents truth and it dispels confusion and evil. A light reveals obstacles that the devil has placed in our path as traps to hurt us. For those who have been in utter darkness, a light gives us great relief. It offers something to focus on so we can set out in the right direction. Jesus was telling us that when we live in and for Him, we radiate His love and grace like a bright light to a world that stumbles around in despair and darkness.

Jesus explains that a light is not to be covered up but set in a prominent place so it can light up a whole room. But then Jesus subtly changes the analogy to tell us we are like a city built on a hill, which can't be hidden. A city, in this case, has influence, meant to be seen and not concealed.

The choice of the word *city* is particularly noteworthy because a city is a collection of people. It's a group. Jesus is saying His disciples are to be a collection of lights. There's a difference in power and radiance between the light of one flashlight and the light of fifty flashlights all bundled together. The more light we put together, the brighter we shine. We become a city on a hill that shines its light to a darkened world.

We see this imagery put into action in Acts 2, where we find a picture of the collective makeup of the early church.

The passage also points to the power of corporate evangelism. (Note that Peter preached to thousands here, so we can see there is a role for large group settings.) At the time, more than three thousand people had become saved. Afterward, the believers began to meet together in the temple courts for further large group teaching, training, and fellowship.

They also met together for deeper fellowship in smaller groups in houses. Notice what happened in those relationships:

> They sold property and possessions to give to anyone who had need. Every day they continued to meet together in the temple courts. They broke bread in their homes and ate together with glad and sincere hearts, praising God and enjoying the favor of all the people. And the Lord added to their number daily those who were being saved. (Acts 2:45–47)

That last line is particularly important to this discussion. *The Lord added to their number daily those who were being saved.* That kind of attraction can happen when individual Christians join together with other Christians in real relationship. We see this picture in Acts of a group of Christians living in Jerusalem, committed to loving God and each other. They had a purpose. The Holy Spirit bound them together and then put them on display for the broken and lonely world to see. They functioned as a city on a hill, a collection of lights.

Paul appeals to the early church in Corinth to live out that kind of unity. In 1 Corinthians 1:10 he writes, "I appeal to you, brothers and sisters, in the name of our Lord Jesus Christ, that all of you agree with one another in what you say and that there be no divisions among you, but that you be perfectly united in mind and thought."

When this Scripture tells us to be "perfectly united," it literally means "knit together." As we read Paul's verse and later passages from the same letter, we learn that we are to be of one mind and heart. We will never fully agree on everything, but we can guard the most important components of our faith together at the head and heart levels. That means we are devoted to one another. We keep our common purpose at the forefront of our thinking and behavior.

Jesus described the benefit that would result from real relationships in John 13:35: "By this everyone will know that you are my disciples, if you love one another." This is how Christians are able to succeed and thrive in a world that is increasingly hostile toward matters of the faith. Not only will relationships help us be stronger in the face of this opposition, but our strength of relationship will attract others who were created to need relationship but can't find it.

Even in a Broken World

Alarming statistics tell us that many who once were church mainstays have stepped away. Also troubling are the statistics that tell us we are losing young people who have grown up in the church. There are a lot of reasons for these losses. The culture, the media, and universities attack Christians' faith. Our youth are often not ready for these attacks because our Christian parents have supported too many extracurricular activities to the detriment of youth group and church services where the Word is taught. Again, most Christian parents were not discipled, so they don't know what it looks like to relationally disciple their own kids. The best many of them can do in their minds is to support extracurricular organizations and activities to keep their children too busy to get into trouble. This of course keeps them too busy to be regularly involved in what the church is doing to reach young people.

But reasons people leave the church extend beyond that. Relationships are like ropes that can keep us fast and hold us strong. Like moorings that hold a boat to the dock, relationships will keep us from drifting away from the truth. Too many times, real relationships aren't there even for those who spend a lot of time at church. Kids have seen their parents bounce from church to church, so the kids grow up never having a real "home" church with real spiritual relationships. Too many youth ministers move on after a short time in one church, so kids go through several youth leaders throughout their growing up years, even if the family stays in one church. Most churches' methodology is pointed toward large, high-energy experiences that don't promote relationship, so most people have acquaintances rather than friendships. This plays a large part in the problem. Without strong ties that bind our kids to other stable believers, our kids are missing an ingredient they need for facing the cultural attacks.

Beyond the miracle of salvation, we are able to have life-giving relationships that Jesus wants to provide. People really can live with understanding, empathy, tenderness, kindheartedness, mercy, and forgiveness toward one another. One of our great miracles is that we really can have relationship both with God and with others. God has given us His directions for this in the Word and has provided power to live it through His Holy Spirit. Only when we follow His directions and walk in His strength will we experience an abundant Christian life.

Sadly though, because few Christians have relationship and are showing others how it's done, most new believers are promised an amazing, abundant life only to receive a weak substitute. Then they leave the church and say they "tried Jesus" but "Jesus didn't really help." That often means they weren't fully plugged in to begin with. They sampled a form of the faith, but it lacked power. To use our ongoing metaphor, they tried to eat what we were cooking, but since we didn't use the right recipe, what we fed them didn't taste very good. They didn't truly see what Jesus can do within a community of believers. Christians cannot leave relationships out of the equation of faith without suffering a large gap between what they have and what they were supposed to have. Without relationships, we are not experiencing the cord of three strands.

Christian relationships should act like ropes that bind us together as we weather life's storms and conquer obstacles. We will not always agree, and there will be conflict, but our commitment to our relationships will keep us constantly moving toward reconciliation, which strengthens us further. At times we will agree to disagree on issues of preference, and other times we will have to submit to people as we seek wise counsel and listen to it.

Life is a battle, but often we avoid the right battles and enter into the wrong ones. When there is conflict, we seek to avoid it, hoping it will go away or decrease in intensity over time. But Scripture tells us we must work together and work through conflict. We must thwart the enemy of relationships from destroying God's good plan for our lives. When we delay dealing with an issue between friends, the enemy gains a foothold and seeks to isolate us so he can break the ropes that bind us.

One of my favorite books is *Sacred Marriage* by Gary Thomas. He makes the point that most people think marriage is to make them *happy*, but, he says, marriage is actually designed to make them *holy*. While my marriage has been filled with many happy times, it's definitely true that God has used Lori to make me holier. The process of sanctification is like the story of the potter and the clay. God has the right to grind us down into powder so He can build us back into a vessel for His good purpose. Or like the gardener in the parable in John 15, God has the right to prune away branches that don't bear fruit. He does this so that we can bear more fruit on productive branches. This process of grinding and pruning is called sanctification, and God exposes our selfishness in relationship and then helps us become more like Him through those same relationships.

Real friendships help us grow up in Christ as we allow people to know us and love us. When we let love be defined by Jesus (meaning we give what others need rather than what they want, and allow them to do the same with us), then relationships can make us not only more fulfilled but also more usable for the Master's good work and glory.

Fellowship Is Actually Worship

A friend from church worked in a restaurant where a cook was experiencing some personal trouble, and my friend asked, "What about God? Have you ever gone to church?"

The cook said, "Nah. I tried that. I went to church once, but it didn't solve my problems. I've never been back since."

The friend said, "Well, what would you think about coming to church again, only this time you come with me?"

The cook thought for a while, then said, "Okay, I guess I could do that."

The cook went to church the next Sunday with my friend. Nothing much seemed to happen that first Sunday, but my friend told me they had talked briefly about something the pastor said. Each week after that, my friend phoned the cook on Saturday night and asked him to go to church. And he did. Weeks went by and the conversations about church and God became more and more relaxed. My friend then asked the cook to come to his home group, but he declined, saying, "I really like you, but some of the people at the church make me nervous." Months went by and the man kept going to church. He eventually agreed to come to home group with my friend after the pastor shared in a sermon about his home group watching sports together. Even though the man wasn't yet a believer, you could tell having friends would mean a lot to him. So he agreed to try the group.

When the man came to the home group he noticed how friendly everyone was. They welcomed each other and him with open hearts, and this was different from what he had expected. Members of the home group shared their lives with each other much more than just once a week, and they would often invite the cook to join them. He was a big baseball fan, so they invited him over to their houses to watch the World Series. Little by little, spiritual conversations were held. The cook noticed the friends in the home group acted differently toward each other. They seemed to really care—both about each other and him, and it wasn't just for show. Once, the cook needed a ride to the airport, so he phoned one of his home group members, who drove him. Another time he was cleaning out his garage, and two of the group members helped him do the job.

The cook found himself involved in their lives too. In the regular home group meetings, they shared things they were going through. He noticed their lives weren't perfect, but they consistently turned to the Lord in prayer and to each other. A year later, when the final game of the World Series was held, the cook held a big party at his house. All his home group members came.

Over time, the home group leader shared the gospel with the cook at a time when he was finally ready to hear it, and soon after that the cook decided to give his life to the Lord.

Just as the early church attracted broken and lonely people through relationship, we are able to do the same today. God designed people to need and desire spiritual meaning and relational connection. People are still people. The world is intrigued when they see real love. Think about it: nearly every song you hear on the radio is about how a person needs love, a real relationship. The problem is that many non-Christians don't think they're going to find real relationships in church. Just like the cook's initial story, they've already "been there, tried that," and it didn't work.

Sure, non-Christians can have relationships with one another, even close relationships, but the goals are different and these relationships don't often make a person safer or better. Typically, without Jesus in the center, a relationship is conditional. It's based upon whether you give me what I think I need. If you make one mistake (or one mistake too many), then you have blown it and the relationship is over. If you don't support me (regardless of whether I am right or my decision is good for anyone), then you are not being a good friend and we are done.

There are exceptions to this rule, of course, and non-Christians can understand forgiveness and reconciliation within relationships. But, again, it's different with Christ at the center. I've lived on both sides of this fence throughout the course of my life. I had seasons of not walking with the Lord, and I've seen people so desperate for relationships they'd give anything for them. I was one of those people. It wasn't that I was physically alone, because often I had many people around me seemingly enjoying life with me, but I was desperately lonely inside. No one really knew what was going on inside of me. Quite frankly, if I were to tell them, their solution would be to offer me another drink, or they would give me a blank stare and have nothing to say because they were dealing with the same problems. When you have Christ as the center of a relationship, you have new depths of grace and help and wisdom and insight and commitment.

It's not that we automatically become great friends the minute we become Christians. The ability to have genuine and deep relationships is part of the sanctification process. Sadly, many Christians are not shown that real sanctification leads to deep relationships, so though they have a form of Christianity, it's not leading them to what they were designed for.

The process is shown in 1 John 4:19: "We love because he first loved us." Before Christ, we had a broken understanding of love because of sin, but now Jesus has revealed real love to us. If you want to know what love looks like, just look at Jesus. Even then, love would be just a nice idea, inaccessible, if Jesus hadn't sent the Holy Spirit, who moves inside of us when we accept Christ. The Holy Spirit enables us to turn the model Christ gave us into more than simply a nice idea. Though we have a sinful nature, with the Holy Spirit's power we can say no to sin and obey Jesus if we choose to. Love takes work. Love takes selflessness. Love involves putting aside our needs and desires for the sake of others. First John 4:7 is clear that we are to love one another because "love comes from God." And 1 John 4:11 adds, "Dear friends, since God so loved us, we also ought to love one another."

These verses hold out an invitation to us, and also a mandate. Since God designed love, and since God speaks the language of love, we are to imitate God and live in this love and let this love flow through us. When we love God and love others the way He commands, we are actually worshiping God. We are also beginning to receive all that God has for us.

You Loved Me Anyway

Friends, one of the best ways to reach lost people is not by shows or big expensive ministry programs. It's by creating atmospheres within our churches that facilitate loving relationships. It's by changing people's lives one person at a time.

This last year we received a letter from a woman I'll call Denise. One of our church women, whom I'll call Susan, had ministered to Denise for many years. Denise had known Susan when she was younger, and she had known Susan was a Christian. But Denise had had no interest in the faith. Although she admitted her friend was genuine and had a life worth desiring, Denise wasn't ready to give up control of her life to Jesus, and she couldn't accept that Jesus could want her after all that had transpired in her life. Denise had made poor choices and also experienced much abuse from those in her physical family who were supposed to love her. Eventually her poor choices had led her to prison. Her life completely unraveled.

When Denise came out of prison, her heart was still hardened, but Susan, along with her home group, decided to pursue Denise and her little daughter anyway. And Susan, who began this process of relational pursuit, needed the help of her spiritual relationships, because as she poured into Denise, she didn't get anything meaningful in return. Often what Denise needed was more than Susan could give alone, so the group of Christians she was in relationship with helped to provide the physical things Denise could not supply by herself. They were also used by the Holy Spirit to pour into her spiritually so she had the strength needed for the long war for Denise's soul.

Unfortunately, Denise wouldn't receive God's love yet, so her fall continued. But the love of Jesus through this group of people also continued. Their pursuit of Denise was not a decision that would lead to immediate results. It would cost them much time and sacrifice.

But eventually it paid off. They ministered to Denise's physical needs and the needs of her daughter even when Denise wasn't grateful and was hurtful, and this eventually softened her heart, and she turned to Jesus. Then Denise wrote this letter to her beloved spiritual mother, Susan, and to our church. This letter is a combination of testimony and poem:

> Ten years ago, yours was the first face I saw when I
>   walked out of prison.
> You knew my infant daughter, but you didn't know
>   me.
> Why would anybody do that?
> I never met anyone like you.
> You invited me to stay with you and your family.
> I ran away. Nobody could love me, and I was proving
>   my lie.
>
> But you loved me anyway.
>
> Your church, Real Life Ministries, was like you. They
>   welcomed and loved.
> I ran away from that too.
> Nobody could love me, and I had to prove my lie.
>
> But you loved me anyway.
>
> I went back to my comfort—what I knew, liked, and
>   was comfortable with.
>
> You were always there, even in my chaos. Oh, the
>   power of a lie.
>
> But you always loved me anyway.
>
> I went back to prison—best thing that ever hap-
>   pened—found an everlasting love, not an idea,
>   found a relationship, not a religion. But also, there
>   you were, faithful, because . . .
>
> You always love me anyway.
>
> Honestly, I don't know my tomorrow story . . .
> But my today story is—

> I'm clean, sober, employed, reconciling with my children, involved in the Real Life Ministries faith community—all because you, your church, your people, disproved my lie. I could be loved.
>
> If I was going to encourage the church, I would say "Keep loving people and don't quit on them!"
>
> I am one who was loved anyway.

That's what the power of real relationships can do. Love makes us stick around others, even when the going gets tough. Love binds us together with other people. Like ropes that hold us fast, love enables us to reach those who are drowning. A drowning man cannot save another drowning man. They both go down. But if a man is drowning and he is thrown a life preserver by someone held fast by many relational ropes, then both can be saved. If still others have blankets and hot coffee ready to warm up the cold swimmers once they're on dry ground, then working together like that they can all save the drowning man and help him learn to live on dry ground.

We so desperately need relationships with other Christians. We journey through life together, and the rough areas of our personalities get sanded away. We are disciples of Christ together, and Jesus transforms us into His image as we yield our lives to Him. Other people are an integral part of the process in our transformation. We become everything Christ wants us to be with the help of real relationships.

As churches, it's so important that we grasp this principle. Real relationship not only builds the opportunity to help someone accept Christ, but it is necessary to help people grow to maturity in Christ. A church is like a family, with

God as the ultimate Father and lesser spiritual parents as our mentors. And still others as our brothers and sisters.

As members of God's family, we must remember that our heavenly Father loves His children intensely. If you ignore or abuse God's children, that doesn't make Him happy. In the family of God, relationships become triangular. God is at the head, and we and other people are on the other two points. When we love others, we also love God. When we help someone who's hungry or needs clothes or companionship, or is sick or in prison, Jesus said it's just like helping Him. In Matthew 25:40 He said, "Truly I tell you, whatever you did for one of the least of these brothers and sisters of mine, you did for me."

As I have written before, when my son Christian was at one of his lowest points with his substance abuse, he needed to be in a rehab center. He didn't last there three days, so the leaders of the center dropped him off at a homeless shelter. Even though it was one of the hardest things my wife and I have ever done, we left him there. He called me from the shelter and asked me to get him out, but I knew he needed to live with his consequences. I couldn't rescue him, and he couldn't live at home and continue to do the things he was doing.

Fortunately, he got serious about recovery. He started going to AA meetings every day, sometimes twice a day. A pastor in town had read some of my books and while serving in the homeless shelter discovered my son was there. This led him to start visiting him once a week, simply to pray for him and minister to him. Sometimes he took him out to lunch. He helped my son get a bike so he could ride to AA meetings that were several miles away. The pastor never once called me to tell me what he was doing. When Christian later told me the pastor was doing this, I was so humbled and grateful. This pastor was doing one of the greatest things he could ever do for me. He was loving my child!

That's how God views it when we care for other people—especially those who have accepted Him and are a part of His spiritual family. It's one of the best things we can ever do for God. The greatest act of worship we can give the Lord is to love those He loves. We love His children. When we minister to other people, we minister to the Lord.

Many other people helped my son too, and there's a reason my son wanted to be in ministry after his life was cleaned up. He'd seen people who would fight for him. When he was down, people helped pick him up. God and God's people brought us through. People prayed for us. They worked with us. They didn't demand that we be perfect. They gave us grace. In a world that's relationally cold because of sin, my son saw warmth, strength, and real love. All those supposed friends he left his parents to please were nowhere to be found when it counted. Yet those whom he had wronged over and over again were there, and it proved to him that what he wanted most he could only find in a spiritual family.

Living Out God's Recipe

Not every story is a success story. As I shared earlier, I grew up in a Christian home. My dad was a pastor, and I saw Christians in both camps. Some Christians were committed to real relationships, but others weren't. Sometimes the people who weren't committed would "overpower" the others. I saw fights in church. I saw people angry at each other, never stopping to work through the conflict. I questioned the effectiveness of the church at that stage of my life, because I saw my dad pouring his life out for other people, but few were pouring back into him. There came a time when I thought my dad was a fool. Too many people had hurt him. Too many people were not committed to the things of Jesus in practice. He was a fool in my eyes because he didn't just walk away from it all. In my mind he was being used.

When I got to college, this hurt was still within me. I wasn't living for the Lord, and sometimes in a class we'd have discussions in which something would be said that would upset the Christians. There were times when I would be ganged up on by those who desired to defend their faith. At this point I loved to see if I could get the Christians to argue with each other, which would take the light off me. I knew the Bible well enough to be able to bait them into arguments. I loved to do that because it proved a point to me. I would try to get them to divide over minor issues of theology, like speaking in tongues or eternal security. Back then those divides between churches were wide, and I knew if I could get them started, then their potential team would disintegrate. Sadly, it often worked.

It took a long while, but eventually I saw that my stereotype of other Christians was wrong. Just because people misrepresent Jesus does not mean Jesus is the problem. While many Christians have missed the point and some Christians genuinely do not get along, many love well.

I eventually came to respect my dad because he and my mother loved others for God's sake even when people didn't deserve this love. I also began to see that what made him and my mom strong were the relationships they had with others—often people I knew nothing about. My dad really was plugged in, but I couldn't see it.

It's true that many people go to church while too few are ever truly a part of it—it's always been this way. These few have the ability to continue God's work with the lost and even eventually win over those whom God plans to break for their own good. The real church will always be those who live out God's recipe for the faith and do it for Jesus's sake no matter what. There will always be seasons when a church catches fire because some of the branches refuse to let their torches go out.

When this happens, a church becomes a city on a hill. We become united on a mission. Because we love God, we love one another, and then other people see this love and are drawn to it.

That's how God designed the church to be.

11

So How Do I Grow Up?

If I could boil all the thoughts in this book down to one idea, it would be this: If we are ever going to grow up in our faith, then we will need spiritual relationships to help us do so. At the same time, our relationships reveal our level of spiritual maturity. A mature person in Christ has deep relationships that help him or her remain mature and even grow further. There is no way to get around the need for real relationships. Scripture teaches this over and over again. Experience bears it out. We must develop, maintain, and champion close relationships with other believers—it's the means to maturity and it's maturity itself.

So what now? Where do we go? What do we do? How do we start?

Many people will want to say, "Yeah, but my church doesn't do this. We don't have small groups." Or "We have small groups, but all we ever do is talk about the Sunday sermon, never about how it applies to our lives." You might say, "No one is real at my church," or "I was real, and shared my struggle, but it only led to gossip." I get that. It can be hard to change a culture that needs to change. But guess what? I'm not asking you to change your church. I'm only asking you to change one person—yourself. I am asking you to face your own fears and have right expectations and start with just you. It won't be easy, and you will get hurt at times, but start with your family and with those who are willing to go with you. If no one is willing to go with you, then it probably means you have some real relational problems that you may not be aware of. So often people decide to check out because the church isn't doing what it's supposed to. They do as I did when I was younger. I blamed other Christians for my lack of obedience to Christ. I blamed others because they didn't want to spend time with me rather than asking the question, How am I acting that might make it difficult to be in relationship with me?

Not long ago I had a conversation with a man who claimed he loved Jesus but he couldn't stand the church. He and his wife were not plugged in anywhere and he self-righteously declared he was within God's will to do as he was doing. So I told him a story.

I asked him to imagine my wife is on her way to church. She parks, gets out of the car, and catches her dress on the door as she gets out. Her dress tears, but she doesn't know it, and with this torn dress she comes walking into church. Parts of her that are not supposed to be seen are visible. What happens? Let's imagine that some people snicker and think my wife looks silly, but they say nothing and continue into the service as if nothing's the matter. Others whisper to their friends or family and point at my wife as she goes by. Let's say some think to themselves, *Well, if this is the way these people dress around here, then I am leaving and not coming back.* But one person sees my wife, quietly walks up to her, and whispers in her ear to tell her that she has torn her dress. At the same time, this person slips his coat off and puts it around my wife to cover the tear.

Certainly my wife has been honored by that person, but here's an additional question: As you think of me as the husband, someone who cares for my wife deeply, which of those people has honored *me* best? Certainly it's the person who showed compassion to my wife, cared for her, and helped her out with her problem.

It's the same way with the church, the beloved bride of Christ. Rather than point at the church and criticize the church for having problems, we should dedicate our lives to sensitively remedying the situation. We don't walk away from the bride with the torn dress and the exposed parts. We're committed to being there for the bride, to helping her be all she can be. Even when she may be exposed on purpose, we care for the bride of Christ because it's the bride of Christ. As the husband of my wife, I can't tell you how much I appreciate the person who seeks to be the solution rather than one who does nothing for (or even worse, speaks poorly of) my wife. This is how Jesus, the Groom of the church, feels about those who seek to remedy broken situations, rather than walk away with pride or disdain. Jesus said blessed are the peacemakers. We so often want to experience peace but don't want to create it through our self-sacrifice and willingness to even suffer through the immaturity of others.

So stay committed to the church, even when problems exist. Now, I am not saying there is not a time to leave, certainly there may be, but wisdom is to know the difference between a salvation issue and a preference issue. Every church has issues because there are people in them, and maturity is to see problems rightly and become a solution if you can. Leaving, as I wrote earlier, should be the last thing you do rather than the first or even second. The church can't be everything to everyone.

Moving toward Maturity

Often people come to our church from other churches. After coming for a while they will tell me they love it here because they are being fed. The obvious implication is that they left the church they had been in because they were not being fed. They believe they are giving me a compliment, but in my mind I am automatically on guard. Why? Because many have left our church for what they say is the same reason. They think they are being spiritual, but in my mind they are revealing their immaturity.

You see, maturity requires you to become a spiritual self-feeder, even if no one around you is. As it pertains to relationship, no pastor can be in relationship with everyone. For a church to have a relational culture, the folks in the church must decide to help create it too. Every person needs spiritual relationship, and they don't need the church to have a program promoting it for it to happen. We are each called to personal responsibility for our own spiritual growth. We each have the capacity to read the Word and see God's design for us within its pages. We have the Holy Spirit inside who can help us live out the Christian walk. We each have the capacity to begin building relationships with other believers without the permission of the pastor and leaders. We may not be able to change the whole culture of a church we attend, but we can create a relational culture for discipleship in our own lives. Often, when a person starts exactly where he is, God steps in and a whole culture is changed just from that little spark that started in the heart of that one person. The place to start is not by abandoning the church. Rather, we are to pray for the church, and to care for the people right around us within the church.

Here's the sequence: We need to start the journey toward maturity ourselves, then help the body of Christ become mature. That should be the goal of every mature Christian. Some people will check out of church because they will not get what they had hoped or expected. They will think of themselves as "victims" and ultimately become critics of the church rather than servants of the body. Self-righteously, they will become those who say the church is immature because it doesn't provide what they think they need—or want. I can't tell you how many times someone has told me I needed to preach on a certain topic because of a particular situation or fascination in their lives. In their minds, the church isn't feeding them, so they insist upon going somewhere they can be fed. After looking around at other churches for a while, they conclude that no one is being fed in them, and they leave the church altogether.

I explain to these types that they are not the only ones in the church, and that others are not dealing with the same issues. I also explain that everything does not need to fit into one spiritual dinner once a week. I explain that everyone is at different stages of spiritual growth and dealing with different things, and that they have a responsibility to learn to feed themselves. They can do studies on particular issues, reading great books on subjects that affect them. They can download sermons from other pastors and listen to them daily. They need to learn to take responsibility for being in relationships where those who are more mature can help feed them.

Often we want to eat a big spiritual meal only once a week, because that is all we want to make time for. But eating one big meal a week to sustain you is not possible physically, and it's not possible spiritually either. Yes, the pastor is responsible to help feed all the people, but that happens not only in Sunday sermons but in relationships built in small groups. Every person is responsible to feed themselves every day if they are to get the spiritual nourishment they need.

Many people check out from the body of Christ because they think they're mature but the church isn't. But if you check out of the church, then you're only showing your spiritual immaturity. The church is God's idea. God loves the church dearly. Yes, we are technically a part of the capital C Church, the universal Church of all believers since the day of Pentecost forward. But people use that theological fact as an excuse not to be a part of the small c church, the local church. Many do this because it allows them to be without any spiritual oversight and accountability. Whether or not they mean to, they are in a dangerous and unproductive place. And we need both the universal and the local.

Since God has so much to say about real relationships in His Word, then we need to listen, regardless if anyone else is or not. Again, I'm not saying that if your church isn't embracing real relationships, you should separate and start your own church. Mature believers understand that we all need to be under authority. Collectively, we are called to do things that we can't do individually. Yet I also recognize individuals should take personal responsibility within the body of Christ. Change starts with me. If I am going to be everything God calls me to be, then I will start to build real relationships. I will be open and honest. I will take the risk. I will be a disciple who allows God to use me to make disciples through the relationships I have right where I am.

People in our sphere of influence will either catch on or shy away. It's true, not everyone jumps on the relationship bandwagon. A lot of Christians are okay with maintaining an isolated, immature spiritual life. It will feel risky for them to begin sharing their lives with others. Or maybe they simply don't know how, so there's a learning curve. Maybe they don't see the benefit, so they refuse to share their lives with anybody. For many, the good things in life take the place of the best things. They will be too busy to commit to real relationships.

But not you. Your life will become different. Even if your church as a whole doesn't embrace real relationships, you can still embrace real relationships yourself. And when the raging cultural river reveals what those around you are riding on (the eight-dollar tube), then you'll be someone who is able to help them out of the river onto a more stable and fulfilling form of flotation.

A Word for the Leaders

Pastors from different churches regularly come to our training seminars. They go through three days of teaching where most of the conversations are about relationships and relational discipleship. Toward the end of their time, they're usually pretty motivated to go back to their churches and see things change. Some pastors are even shaken up. Why? Because they now realize they don't have real friendships in their church. This has been revealed over our time together. At the beginning of the week, we asked everyone if they had a good friend, and almost all raised their hand. We then started to help them define what a close friendship looks like from a biblical perspective. A close friend is someone you spend time with consistently. You can tell this person your fears, confess your sins and struggles, allow yourself to be held accountable to any changes you discover you need to make. Your time together is not like a counseling session, but there's no pretending, no hiding, no secret-keeping. You pray together. You go to Scripture together about issues that arise. The person cares about you no matter your flaws, no matter what you do for a living, regardless of how much money you make or don't make.

And the friendship goes both ways. The other person shares his or her life with you too.

As we define this, the pastors will often say something like, "Oh, that's my wife." Or, "Oh yeah, I had a friend like that thirty years ago, but not so much today in my church." Sometimes they'll talk about a golfing buddy. Or a colleague they met at a pastors' conference. But then we'll talk about how there's a difference between *being* a friend and *having* a friend. A lot of these leaders will minister to the people around them, but if they themselves are hurting, they don't blow the trumpet that sounds the alarm. They're always being poured out, but they're not being poured into.

I say all this to note that I see a lot of lonely pastors come to our seminars. And lonely pastors tend to create lonely churches. Lonely pastors are not only outside real relationships themselves, but they create a culture where mature disciples are not made, because of course mature disciples are not lonely.

I've seen this worldwide. I've seen this all over North America. I've seen this in Africa and India. Even in places where people live twenty to a house. People might be confined in physically close quarters, but that doesn't necessarily mean they're doing life together, sharing struggles and triumphs, praying for each other, and walking the journey together.

We went to India last year on a ministry trip for pastoral leaders, and after several days of talking about relational discipleship with hundreds of pastors, we were privileged to meet with the key leaders in a closed small group session. It was a chance to be real with men who thought they knew each other. I began by sharing some of my past and current struggles, and then gave them the opportunity to be honest as well. Few in the group would say anything on the first day. They wouldn't be open. They weren't used to talking that way with anybody, not even in a communal culture. The older leaders were the most closed. They'd talk about Scripture, and they'd give examples from their congregations of how people's physical needs were being met, but none would talk about their personal lives.

I asked the question several times over several days, and from different angles. Finally, one younger leader spoke up and said, "Okay, here's the truth. I believe you are asking us where we are personally. Is this correct?"

I said, "Exactly."

"All right. In our culture, women will bathe in a river publicly. You drive by, and they're washing in the river. I struggle with lust—and I need prayer."

The air went out of the room.

Then one or two of the older ones opened up. The atmosphere changed, and suddenly we were talking about real issues. One was angry with his wife, another had a son who had left the faith and he felt condemnation and was thinking about quitting the ministry altogether. Some were shocked by the struggles others were having because their lives had always seemed perfect. We were on our way to real sanctification and real spiritual maturity. As they experienced the freedom to share and the encouragement it brought, they began to ask, "How can we get our churches to change in this area? How can we get our people to be in real relationship with one another?"

I said, "I'm not asking how to change your church. I'm asking how you can change yourself. It starts with you. You must see in God's Word that we are clearly called to be in relationships with one another. Spiritual maturity is developed within relationships. So if this is true, and if I don't have relationships, then there must be a change of heart and repentance."

This is true of any Christian, leader or not. If I want to begin on a road to spiritual maturity, then I must see the need for real relationships as defined in Scripture.

Like the House on the Rock

I find that the people who often have the hardest time becoming relational are those who have been in church a long time.

If you ask personal questions, they don't want to talk. They will often point to the Bible and say, "This is all we need for spiritual growth. Read it. Study it. Learn it."

I'd say yes to all of that, but I'd add one important thing: *Live it in relationship.*

Yes, we must immerse ourselves in Scripture. We must read Scripture and study Scripture and memorize Scripture and be able to run it forward and backward in our minds. First Peter 2:2 says, "Like newborn babies, crave pure spiritual milk, so that by it you may grow up in your salvation." Here we see a direct correlation between God's Word and growing up in our salvation. Yet Peter isn't saying that merely knowing the Word will grow us up. Knowledge of Scripture without application does nothing. We can study the context and learn the Greek and Hebrew and even memorize a passage backward and forward, but Scripture indicates that the Word must be acted out too. James 1:22 says, "Do not merely listen to the word, and so deceive yourselves. Do what it says."

Jesus gave a series of teachings in Matthew 7 about being both hearers and doers of the Word. Notice the teaching woven into the parable of the house on the rock.

> Therefore everyone who hears these words of mine and puts them into practice is like a wise man who built his house on the rock. The rain came down, the streams rose, and the winds blew and beat against that house; yet it did not fall, because it had its foundation on the rock. But everyone who hears these words of mine and does not put them into practice is like a foolish man who built his house on sand. The rain came down, the streams rose, and the winds blew and beat against that house, and it fell with a great crash. (Matt. 7:24–27)

That's clear. If you hear the words of God and put them into practice, then your life will be like that of a man who built his house on a foundation of rock. But if you hear the words of God and don't put them into practice, then your life will be like that of a man who built his house on sand. Wisdom is contrasted with foolishness. Spiritual maturity is contrasted with spiritual immaturity. Great benefit is contrasted with destruction.

The problem is that too many Christians have built their houses on sand or a combination of sand and rock. They are missing an important ingredient in their spiritual lives. They have no real relationships, no ropes that hold them fast. A house built on sand can't withstand pressure. When the rain and wind come—the enticements of the culture, the lusts of the flesh, the pride of life, the snares of addictions—those houses built on sand will collapse.

Model the Humility and Love of Christ

So, how do we grow up?

Ultimately, the only way to truly grow is by abiding in Christ and obeying his commands. This connection with Jesus must be established first. By God's grace we must continually draw nearer to the Lord. John 15:4–5 (NASB) is the core passage that teaches this. Jesus says to His disciples,

> Abide in Me, and I in you. As the branch cannot bear fruit of itself unless it abides in the vine, so neither can you unless you abide in Me. I am the vine, you are the branches; he who abides in Me and I in him, he bears much fruit, for apart from Me you can do nothing.

The word *abide* is *menō* in the Greek. It means to live, to continue, to endure, to stay, to remain as one, to be kept continually in position. When we abide with Christ, we live in Christ. We stay close to Christ. We allow the Holy Spirit to draw our minds and hearts close to the mind and heart of Christ.

Paul teaches a similar concept in Galatians 2:20 when he says, "I have been crucified with Christ; and it is no longer I who live, but Christ lives in me; and the life which I now live in the flesh I live by faith in the Son of God, who loved me and gave Himself up for me" (NASB). This is a picture of a person "abiding" in Christ. Paul acknowledges that his personal will is gone by choice. His personal opinion doesn't matter anymore. The only thing that matters anymore is Christ. This verse acknowledges that Jesus actually lives and works inside a believer. But we must choose daily to follow Jesus, and this isn't a one-time decision. Jesus tells us we must daily take up our cross and follow Him. Every day my flesh (old nature) is right there with me, and I must choose to say no to it and follow Jesus. Your flesh in control for one hour can damage your life for years. This concept of abiding means a continuing decision to listen and obey Jesus through His Word.

John teaches a similar concept in 1 John 3:24: "The one who keeps His commandments abides in Him, and He in him. We know by this that He abides in us, by the Spirit whom He has given us" (NASB). Ask yourself, what are the commandments of Jesus? Clearly, the most important commandments are to love God and to love others. More than that, all the commandments hang on these commands. In other words, the commandments promote and protect relationship. So according to this verse, when we do this, we can have confidence that Jesus abides in us and we abide in Jesus.

How do we grow up?

We abide in Christ, because apart from Him we can do nothing. We learn to feed ourselves spiritually. What do we feed on? We feed on the spiritual meal described in Scripture—His recipe, not one of our own making. His recipe includes spiritual relationships with other believers.

Do you remember the story of the Last Supper? It begins with the scene of Jesus washing the disciples' feet. John 13:1–17 says,

> It was just before the Passover Festival. Jesus knew that the hour had come for him to leave this world and go to the Father. Having loved his own who were in the world, he loved them to the end.
>
> The evening meal was in progress, and the devil had already prompted Judas, the son of Simon Iscariot, to betray Jesus. Jesus knew that the Father had put all things under his power, and that he had come from God and was returning to God; so he got up from the meal, took off his outer clothing, and wrapped a towel around his waist. After that, he poured water into a basin and began to wash his disciples' feet, drying them with the towel that was wrapped around him.
>
> He came to Simon Peter, who said to him, "Lord, are you going to wash my feet?"
>
> Jesus replied, "You do not realize now what I am doing, but later you will understand."
>
> "No," said Peter, "you shall never wash my feet."
>
> Jesus answered, "Unless I wash you, you have no part with me."

"Then, Lord," Simon Peter replied, "not just my feet but my hands and my head as well!"

Jesus answered, "Those who have had a bath need only to wash their feet; their whole body is clean. And you are clean, though not every one of you." For he knew who was going to betray him, and that was why he said not every one was clean.

When he had finished washing their feet, he put on his clothes and returned to his place. "Do you understand what I have done for you?" he asked them. "You call me 'Teacher' and 'Lord,' and rightly so, for that is what I am. Now that I, your Lord and Teacher, have washed your feet, you also should wash one another's feet. I have set you an example that you should do as I have done for you. Very truly I tell you, no servant is greater than his master, nor is a messenger greater than the one who sent him. Now that you know these things, you will be blessed if you do them."

The example of Jesus is to adopt the position of a servant. This is the attitude of love. Jesus took off his outer clothing, wrapped a towel around his waist, poured water into a basin, and began to wash the disciples' feet. This event is a beautiful picture of abiding in Christ.

We know we must continually allow Jesus to wash us—even our most disgusting filth. Dirt was everywhere in that period of time, and people wore open-toed sandals. Whenever they traveled or walked anywhere, their feet became filthy. Servants were responsible for washing the feet of guests, not only as a sign of respect and hospitality, but also because of hygiene issues. So Jesus was giving a physical illustration to reveal a spiritual reality. Jesus came to wash away the filthiest parts of our lives. The parts that are most attached to the physical world we live in. And we must let Him do it. If we refuse, we cannot be saved. This passage reveals the heart of our amazing God. He is willing to come down and clean up our messes—that blows me away.

But there's more. Remember that Jesus said we are to wash each other's feet as He has done for us. Jesus used a physical illustration to reveal a spiritual truth. We are to uncover our feet (our filthiest parts) to those we are in spiritual relationship with. We are not to hide our dirt, but allow others to see it and even help us clean it up. We are to do the same for others.

And feet washing doesn't happen just once. Filth finds its way onto our feet over and over again as we pass through this broken world. Jesus did not come to die only for our past sins. He continues to clean us even as we go through life. He continues to pour grace into our lives. Grace and forgiveness are not one-time things but are continually being poured into our lives by Jesus. We continue to struggle and we continue to need grace. First John 1:8–9 tells us that if we claim we are without sin we are liars, but if we confess our sin He is faithful and just to forgive us of all unrighteousness. Jesus came to wash our sin away, and we must let Him.

This passage reveals that we all have a part in helping each other through relationship to wash one another's feet. Many, like the Pharisees, completely miss the point of what God is saying through His Word and the actions of Christ Jesus. I know of many churches that have foot washing ceremonies but will not make the connection to the deeper point. Feet are personal, and can be one of the ugliest parts of our bodies. They are the parts of our body that have constant connection with the world, and they take the greatest wear and tear. We are to reveal to each other our personal struggles and our failings. James said it this way—we confess our sins one to another, praying so we can be healed. We are honest and allow each other to reveal the inner struggles. Rather than cover our noses at the stink of spiritual feet, we take on the role of servant to help clean up the mess. And we allow others to do the same for us.

What a beautiful picture of how we are both cleansed by the work of Jesus and helped along the way through acts of transparency and servanthood.

Your Choice Today

Last week I was deeply affected by another friend who confessed that he had had an affair. He "had" to confess it, because he had been caught. Now his wife is devastated, and his children are confused and hurt. He is a fairly prominent person in our community and well known for claims of being a Christian. In the last several years, I have had many conversations with him about his need to do more than go to church on the weekends. He always told me his walk with God was fine and that he was too busy with his small children and their sports. Or his business was "just too crazy." He never had time for real relationships.

Sadly, most of the things that kept him from real relationship with people who would help and protect him are very possibly going to be gone from his life. Now he has time to do the things he was asked to do, but it may be too late to save his marriage. His reputation has now been soiled, and the reputation of the Lord has been affected too. Fortunately, he is seeking God's plan for his life now, but if you were to ask him in hindsight what he would have done differently, what do you think he would say?

People who have decided to prioritize abiding in Christ and deep relationships with others will wisely avoid so much pain. Unfortunately for those who don't abide, sooner or later this disconnect from God's recipe for the spiritual life will affect their spiritual walks in significant ways. I am not saying every person will have an affair or derail their lives, but many will end up having far less than they were designed to have.

To choose something other than God's best always comes with some kind of negative consequences. What a shame to miss out on God's design. To live out His great recipe for the spiritual life does not mean that you will have no issues. Jesus made it clear that even the house on the rock will have wind and rain beat against it. But God promises that a house built by His design will not only survive the storm but will thrive.

As I close this book, let's think again of the eight-dollar Walmart tube needing to carry its rider through a class V rapids run. Here is truth: We are all called to grow to maturity. Maturity in Christ has several components—understanding the Word and obeying its standards of morality, understanding our giftedness and purpose, having a strong prayer life, keeping our commitment to Christ even if it means suffering, and leading with strong character are all a part of maturity. But maturity also entails our ability to love and to be loved. The turbulent river is a picture of life, and we have to admit that our culture is going crazy and we don't ride an easygoing, meandering, relaxing river anymore. The world around us really is in class V rapids, and if we are to get down the river successfully we are going to need more than an eight-dollar Walmart tube. If our families and churches are to thrive, let alone survive, we will need to be in properly equipped, trained teams who care about one another and work together to get down this river.

It is my prayer that you will trade in your inadequate tube for God's better plan. Then you can experience the faith life God designed you to have.

Acknowledgments

Huge thanks to the church family, staff, and elders of Real Life Ministries. My wife, Lori, and all our family and friends. Agent Greg Johnson of the WordServe Literary Group. My writing partner, Marcus Brotherton. Brian Thomasson and the team at Baker Publishing Group.

Jim Putman is the founder and senior pastor of Real Life Ministries in Post Falls, Idaho.

Real Life Ministries began as a small group in 1998 and has grown to a membership of more than eight thousand people. The church was launched with a commitment to discipleship and the model of discipleship Jesus practiced, which is called "Relational Discipleship." Ninety percent of the people are active in small groups. *Outreach Magazine* continually lists Real Life Ministries among the top one hundred most influential churches in America.

Jim is also the founding leader of the new Relational Discipleship Network. Jim holds degrees from Boise State University and Boise Bible College. Each year his teaching ministry reaches hundreds of thousands across the nation through speaking conferences, the web, radio, and weekend services.

He is the author of three books: *Church Is a Team Sport*, *Real Life Discipleship*, and *Real Life Discipleship Workbook* (with Avery Willis and others).

Jim's passion is discipleship through small groups. With his background in sports and coaching, he believes in the value of strong coaching as a means to disciple others.

He lives with his wife and three sons in scenic northern Idaho.

Real Life Ministries is a nondenominational Evangelical Christian church in northern Idaho. The church was planted in 1998 by four families, including senior pastor Jim Putman, and has grown quickly. The vision of Real Life Ministries is to reach the world for Jesus one person at a time by making biblical disciples in relational environments.

We would love to have you join us at one of our small groups, weekend services, or special events!

@RLM_Lifer

Real Life Ministries

@RLMLifer

Real Life Ministries

To learn more, visit

RealLifeMinistries.com

ALSO BY
JIM PUTMAN

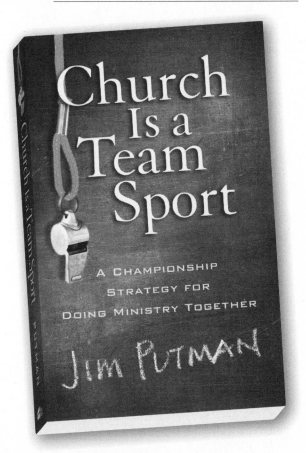

Church Is a Team Sport demonstrates proven coaching strategies to inspire believers to grow as a team of Christians and leaders. In his straightforward, compelling style, pastor Jim Putman will help you discover authentic discipleship that changes lives and equips every member of your church to be a motivated follower of Jesus Christ.

LIKE THIS
BOOK?
Consider sharing it with others!

- Share or mention the book on your social media platforms. Use the hashtag **#PowerofTogether**.

- Write a book review on your blog or on a retailer site.

- Pick up a copy for friends, family, or strangers! Anyone who you think would enjoy and be challenged by its message.

- Share this message on Twitter or Facebook: **"I loved #PowerofTogether by @JimPutmanRLM //** RealLifeMinistries.com @ReadBakerBooks."

- Recommend this book for your church, workplace, book club, or class.

- Follow Baker Books on social media and tell us what you like.

 Facebook.com/ReadBakerBooks

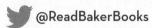 @ReadBakerBooks